The Four Shakespeare Folios

The Four Shakespeare Folios

Copy, Print, Paper, Type

EDITED BY SAMUEL V. LEMLEY

The Pennsylvania State University Press
University Park, Pennsylvania

Carnegie Mellon University Libraries
Pittsburgh, Pennsylvania

Library of Congress
Cataloging-in-Publication Data

Names: Lemley, Samuel V. (Samuel Vincent), editor.
Title: The four Shakespeare folios : copy, print, paper, type / [edited by] Samuel V. Lemley.
Other titles: Penn State series in the history of the book.
Description: University Park, Pennsylvania : The Pennsylvania State University Press ; Pittsburgh, Pennsylvania : Carnegie Mellon University Libraries, [2024] | Series: The Penn State series in the history of the book | Includes bibliographical references and index.
Summary: "A collection of essays by leading scholars of Shakespeare in print, offering an overview of current research on the Folios and on unsettled questions about the bibliography of Shakespeare's plays"— Provided by publisher.
Identifiers: LCCN 2024000835 | ISBN 9780271097329 (cloth)
Subjects: LCSH: Shakespeare, William, 1564–1616—Bibliography—Folios. | LCGFT: Essays.
Classification: LCC Z8813 F68 2024 | DDC 016.8223/3—dc23/eng/20240205
LC record available at https://lccn.loc.gov/2024000835

Copyright © 2024 Carnegie Mellon University
All rights reserved
Printed in the United States of America
Published by The Pennsylvania State University Press, University Park, PA 16802–1003

The Pennsylvania State University Press is a member of the Association of University Presses.

It is the policy of The Pennsylvania State University Press to use acid-free paper. Publications on uncoated stock satisfy the minimum requirements of American National Standard for Information Sciences—Permanence of Paper for Printed Library Material, ANSI Z39.48–1992.

CONTENTS

List of Illustrations | vii
Foreword by Keith Webster | xi
Acknowledgments | xv

Introduction | 1
Samuel V. Lemley

1 Publishing the Four Folios | 13
Andrew Murphy

2 Paper, Type, and Labor: Making the First Folio | 33
Claire M. L. Bourne

3 The Droeshout Portrait and the Title Page | 59
Erin C. Blake

4 "Folio" and Format: Supersizing Shakespeare | 77
Tara L. Lyons

5 Surviving Shakespeare: Or, What We Can Learn from 3,000 Copies and 382 Fragments of the Plays and Poems | 95
Zachary Lesser

6 Everything There Is to Be Learned About Seventeenth-Century Types: Computational Bibliography and the Fourth Folio's Printers | 117
Samuel V. Lemley, Nikolai Vogler, Christopher N. Warren, D. J. Schuldt, Laura S. DeLuca, Kari Thomas, Taylor Berg-Kirkpatrick, Elizabeth Dieterich, Kartik Goyal, Max G'Sell

Reference List | 145
List of Contributors | 153
Index | 157

ILLUSTRATIONS

i.1. The two states of the Third Folio's title page | 6
i.2. The inscribed names of Alice and Margaret Brownlowe | 8
i.3. Henry Tilson, portrait of Margaret Brownlowe | 9
1.1. The colophon included at the end of the First Folio | 17
1.2. John Smethwick credited as publisher on an individual title page of the Second Folio | 22
1.3. Robert Allot credited as publisher on the title page of a copy of the Second Folio | 22
1.4. The opening page of *Much Ado About Nothing* in the First Folio | 24
1.5. The opening page of *Much Ado About Nothing* in the Second Folio | 25
1.6. The title page of the second issue of the Third Folio | 27
1.7. Opening of the Fourth Folio | 29
1.8. A sample opening of one of the pages included in the so-called "Fifth Folio" | 30
2.1. The First Folio was structured as a series of gatherings of three sheets (or six leaves, or twelve pages) | 35
2.2. All inked characters feature a raised face (here, "A") on top of a metal alloy body | 39
2.3. Type from a font was organized and stored in upper and lower cases | 40
2.4. Compositors used a composing stick to set type before transferring it to the galley | 41
2.5. A quarto forme locked up for printing | 41
2.6. The first opening (two-page spread) of the First Folio | 43
2.7. The page of the First Folio's prefatory matter | 44
2.8. The first page of *Henry the Sixth, Part 1* | 45
2.9. A page from *A Midsummer Night's Dream* | 46
2.10. The design of the final pages of three playtexts | 47
2.11. John Milton's copy of the First Folio | 48
2.12. Error in running title for *The Merry Wives of Windsor* | 54
2.13. *King Lear* with supplemented *E* from another typeface | 57
3.1. Title page of *The Workes of Benjamin Jonson* | 60

3.2. Frontispiece and title page of *The Workes of the Most High and Mightie Prince, James* | 61
3.3. Jan van der Straet, "Impressio librorum," from *Nova Reperta* | 62
3.4. Woodcut title page of Thomas Middleton and William Rowley, *The World Tost at Tennis* | 63
3.5. Jan van der Straet, "Sculptura in aes," from *Nova Reperta* | 65
3.6. Title page of the First Folio | 66
3.7. Details from the first, second, third, and fourth states of the Droeshout portrait | 70
3.8. Title page of *The Prophecies of the Twelve Sybills* | 71
3.9. Frontispiece and title page of the First Folio | 73
3.10. Frontispiece and title page of the 1664 Third Folio | 74
4.1. Title page of the First Folio and title page of Shakespeare's *The Merry Wives of Windsor* (1619) | 78
4.2. The First Folio, page 391 | 81
4.3. Jonson's *Works* (1616), page 211 | 83
4.4. Title page of the Third Folio | 86
4.5. The Four Shakespeare Folios in sequence from left to right | 89
4.6. Title page of the Fourth Folio | 90
4.7. Bentley's Catalogue of Plays | 92
5.1. A copy of the First Folio at the Folger Shakespeare Library | 96
5.2. The only surviving evidence for the tenth edition of *Venus and Adonis* | 99
5.3. The First Folio now at the University of Padova, marked up for performance | 103
5.4. A page from *All's Well That Ends Well* in a Second Folio that was censored | 104
5.5. A reader of this First Folio at Meisei University in Japan made extensive notes | 107
5.6. The signatures of Alice Brownlowe (1659–1721) and her daughters | 109
5.7. Frances Wolfreston's ownership mark and comment on her copy of the 1655 *Othello* | 109
5.8. A composite created by patching the Second Folio title page with newly printed sections | 112
5.9. A hand-drawn facsimile title page by John Harris | 113
6.1. Hamlet, "rpince of denmark" | 118
6.2. A digitally reconstructed broken uppercase *R* | 120
6.3. Damaged type algorithmically harvested from the Fourth Folio | 122
6.4. A functioning Hinman Collator | 124

6.5. The "crudely-cut floral initial" *B* in *Scornful Lady* (1677) and the same initial *B* on page 1 of the Fourth Folio | 129

6.6. Title page, *Annotations upon the Holy Bible* | 131

6.7. Fourth Folio title page, *Mr. William Shakespear's Comedies, Histories, and Tragedies* | 132

6.8. The distinctively damaged *L* and *Y* | 133

6.9. Inked flecks of type metal or debris visible in both impressions of the damaged *Y* | 133

6.10. A table showing Fourth Folio-to-Everingham matches | 134

6.11. A table of distinctively damaged types that appear in the Fourth Folio | 137

6.12. A distinctively damaged titling *R* | 138

6.13. A distinctively damaged titling *Y* | 139

6.14. The Knight-Saunders state of the Fourth Folio's title page | 140

6.15. Matches in the Fourth Folio part 2 (printed by Everingham) and the reprinted "Fifth Folio" sheets | 141

FOREWORD

William Shakespeare left an indelible mark on the literary world with his profound insights into the human condition. His works have endured for centuries, captivating audiences and scholars alike. However, the preservation, interpretation, and dissemination of Shakespeare's plays and poetry would not have been possible without the expertise of generations of librarians. Libraries play an instrumental role in preserving Shakespeare's works. Over time, countless libraries have acquired rare and early editions of his plays, ensuring their longevity for future generations. These libraries serve as custodians of literary treasures, meticulously preserving and protecting the delicate manuscripts and printed editions from decay and loss. Their efforts allow scholars to study the evolution of Shakespeare's texts, comparing different editions or copies and uncovering nuances within the plays.

Libraries provide a haven for scholars seeking to deepen their understanding and advance their scholarship. Collections of critical editions, commentaries, and scholarly publications create fertile ground for research and intellectual exploration. Academic scholars benefit immensely from libraries' extensive resources, which enable them to scrutinize and analyze Shakespeare's works from various perspectives, such as literary, historical, and cultural contexts. By availing themselves of these resources, scholars gain valuable insights into the intricate themes, characters, and linguistic mastery that define Shakespeare's canon.

Further, libraries serve as vibrant intellectual hubs where scholars and researchers can collaborate. They frequently host conferences, seminars, and lectures that support the exchange of ideas and foster interdisciplinary approaches to studying Shakespeare. Scholars from diverse disciplines, such as literature, theater, history, and linguistics, come together within library walls to share their research and point to new avenues of inquiry. The dynamic environment of libraries nurtures scholarly dialogue, pushing the boundaries of Shakespeare studies. Current technological work in fields of artificial intelligence, machine learning, and virtual and augmented reality all offer powerful new approaches to advancing understanding.

In this digital age, when almost all new scholarly content arrives in our libraries in digital form it is tempting to question the need to celebrate the four-hundredth anniversary of a book the contents of which are freely available to anyone with an internet connection. The digital shift of the past twenty-five years, and especially the acceleration in demand for online materials seen during the COVID-19 pandemic, must surely consign the physical book into the realms of history?

Such a view, of course, misses the point. In an age where contemporary library collections are increasingly homogenous, it is special collections of rare and distinctive materials that mark a library's competitive edge. Traditionally, libraries were a critical force in advancing their institutions. Simplistically, great collections attracted scholars who, in turn, would gather the scholars and collaborators to attract research funding. In turn, this would support further investment in collections, creating an upward spiral of excellence. In the digital realm, this model of collections and scholarship has largely had its day, and it is a library's special collections that allow for a measure of distinctiveness. Carefully curated collections of rare books, so designated by virtue of age or value, and associated artifacts, truly offer a measure of distinctiveness that can attract and nurture scholarship.

It is notable that the vast majority of surviving copies of Shakespeare's Folios, and especially the First, are housed in libraries. For centuries, librarians have created conditions in which the collections in their charge might survive threats of flood, fire, and infestation. That we are able to celebrate the four-hundredth anniversary of the First Folio with so many copies surviving is a tribute to generations of dedicated stewards.

Of course, few libraries have the resources with which to acquire the rarest of materials. Many of our collections have been built upon the generous support of donors and philanthropists. Their motivations vary—some wish their books to be given the expert stewardship offered by librarians, others wish to advance scholarship by offering the widest possible access to their collections, and others wish to leave a legacy. These benefactors achieve another outcome—demonstrating access to knowledge. For some, the simple provision of access might be the only means through which a scholar could read a work. In other cases, while a text may be widely available through reprints and special editions, it is the special story told by an individual copy of a book that is significant.

A new wave of democratization has emerged in the digital age. Libraries play a crucial role in making Shakespeare's works accessible to a diverse audience. Through their lending programs, digitization initiatives, and educational outreach, libraries ensure that Shakespeare's plays are available to all, transcending geographical and socioeconomic barriers. Libraries have embraced technology to create digital repositories, making rare materials and critical editions accessible online. This democratization of knowledge empowers scholars and enthusiasts worldwide to engage with Shakespeare's works, fostering a global community of Shakespeare scholars and enthusiasts.

Shakespeare's enduring literary legacy owes a great debt to libraries. These repositories of knowledge serve as guardians, scholars, and disseminators of the Bard's works. Through their preservation efforts, extensive resources, archival collections, and commitment to accessibility, libraries ensure that Shakespeare's genius continues to captivate and inspire academic scholars. As we celebrate Shakespeare's profound impact on literature, theater, and humanity, we must acknowledge the invaluable role libraries play in safeguarding and promoting his works.

Keith Webster
Helen and Henry Posner, Jr. Dean of the University Libraries
Carnegie Mellon University

ACKNOWLEDGMENTS

The editor is grateful to the following for their assistance on this publication: Patrick H. Alexander, Elizabeth Barker, Heidi Wiren Bartlett, Dawn Reid Brean, Maddie Caso, Matthew D'Emilio, Blair Dunckel, Josie DiNovo, Jim Garrett and the Carnegie Mellon University Office of the Provost, Gretchen Graff, Kevin Lorenzi, Ann Marie Mesco, Joseph Mesco, Janice North, Jennifer Norton, Gretchen Otto, Joelle Pitts, The Posner Fine Arts Foundation, Alex Ramos, Shannon Riffe, Ken Rose, Joanna Steinhardt, and Morgan Walbert.

Introduction

Samuel V. Lemley

The word *folio* appears only once in Shakespeare's plays.* In the final lines of the first act of *Love's Labour's Lost*, a comedy, Don Adriano de Armado invokes the instruments of his literary art: "Devise wit, write pen, for I am for whole volumes in folio." The reference is not a flattering one. Armado is a braggart, enamored of his own stilted way of speaking, and his oath to fill folios with the strained devising of his wit is not one we hope he keeps. The irony is that a play concerned with literary fame—that elusive object that can "make us heirs of all eternity," according to the King (1.1.7)—puts *folio*, the word perhaps most closely tied to Shakespeare's own literary legacy, in the mouth of one of Shakespeare's most mercilessly rendered fools.

Strictly speaking, "folio" describes a bibliographic format, or shape of book: early printed books were made up of sheets of paper that, once printed, gathered, and folded, were stitched together in sequence and bound into volumes. A folio is simply a book made up of sheets of paper folded once, making two leaves and four pages, usually of a large size (see Claire M. L. Bourne's chapter in this book, and especially fig. 2.1). But *folio* is more than a term of art. When Shakespeare's acting company, the Lord Chamberlain's Men, first performed *Love's Labour's Lost* in 1594, *folio* was already a word with considerable cultural freighting. And

---

* Thanks to Claire M. L. Bourne for this observation.

by the end of the seventeenth century, as Francis X. Connor has observed, folios could represent "completeness, cultural prominence, and . . . literary immortality"—a fitting target, in other words, for Shakespeare's satire and an apt vessel for Armado's literary pretensions (Connor 2014, 177). But for Shakespeare, the word has accrued other, more specific meanings. *Mr. William Shakespeares Comedies, Histories, & Tragedies*, more widely known as the First Folio, contains thirty-six of the thirty-eight plays attributed in whole or in part to Shakespeare—that is, those written either by himself or in collaboration with other playwrights. When it was issued from the London print shop of Isaac Jaggard in November, 1623, the Folio represented the first successful attempt to gather Shakespeare's dramatic corpus in one volume. And despite the fact that it was published posthumously, without Shakespeare's involvement, the First Folio has attained a kind of mythic status: if folios stand for completeness, cultural prominence, and literary immortality, the First Folio typifies the format. Standing first for completeness (its editors, the actors John Heminge and Henry Condell, claimed in their preface to have gathered the plays and printed them "absolute in their numbers, as [Shakespeare] conceived them"), it has since become perhaps the most culturally prominent book in the English-speaking world and now functions as a byword for Shakespeare's literary immortality.

Why, then, does this book, a volume of admittedly slighter dimensions than most folios, consider all four Shakespeare Folios instead of the First alone? Call it an attempt at a corrective. There exists in Shakespeare studies—or at least has existed until recently—an enduring fixation on origins: the authorship and origin of individual plays (so-called attribution studies), the origins of Shakespeare's plots (which Shakespeare often borrowed and only rarely invented), and the textual origins of Shakespeare in print. In this last category, the Folio has loomed large: of the thirty-six plays it contains, eighteen were printed in no other edition. This means that without the Folio, these eighteen plays—including *The Tempest*, *Julius Caesar*, and *Macbeth*—would have been lost, and the Shakespeare canon would be reduced by half. Because of this, three subsequent Shakespeare folios—a Second, printed in 1632, a Third printed in 1663, and a Fourth printed in 1685—have, as Jeffrey Todd Knight recently put it, long inhabited "a critic's no-man's land" (2017, 4). The later folios were textually negligible, mere derivatives of the First. And worse than that, each subsequent Folio muddled the First with textual impurities consequent to their printers' ignorance or carelessness. The later Folios thus carried, according to Fredson Bowers, bibliographer and Shakespeare scholar, no authority in the editing of Shakespeare's plays (1951, 241). Stanley Wells's *An A–Z Guide to Shakespeare* (Oxford 2013) follows suit and describes the later folios as "reprints [with] no independent authority"

(Wells 2013). More recently scholars have troubled this account with new evidence, but the premise holds: the First Folio's proximity to Shakespeare and to those who knew him lends it an authority that the later folios lack. Enshrining this notion, one exhibition held to mark the four-hundredth anniversary of Shakespeare's death in 2016 described the First Folio as "the book that gave us Shakespeare" ("First Folio!").

This idea has a long history. Samuel Johnson—the eighteenth-century lexicographer and famously voluble subject of James Boswell's *Life*—suggested that "the first [Folio] is equivalent to all others, and the rest only deviate from it by the printer's negligence. Whoever has any of the folios has all, excepting those diversities which mere reiteration of editions will produce" (quoted in Murphy 2021, 112). George Steevens, who edited Shakespeare's plays with Johnson, was even more dismissive, likening the later folios to "mere waste paper" (quoted in Hooks 2016, 190). Implied by Johnson and Steeven's language is the idea of sameness, even equivalence between the Folios, and a generally untroubled sequence that led from the First to the Fourth. The chapters in this book trouble this idea, finding alterations, both profound and subtle, made between and within each edition and argue instead for a composite view of the four Folios.

In treating the histories of the Shakespeare Folios under a shared heading, this book seeks to modify the view that the survival of Shakespeare's plays was due solely, or even primarily, to the survival of the First Folio (228 complete copies of which are extant). Rather, the survival of the plays—that is, their continued reception by new and increasingly varied communities of readers—is due also to the fact that the Folio was reprinted in three subsequent editions. The four Folios, all published in the seventeenth century, stand for Shakespeare's appeal in the period, and each contributed to the gradual elevation of Shakespeare in the English literary canon. It is fitting, then, that a short poem by John Milton that describes the Folio and its contents as "a lasting Monument" was printed in the opening pages of the Second Folio (1632) and not the First. In other words, literary legacy is a fragile thing made durable by reprinting. Yet the 2023 publication of Chris Laoutaris's book *Shakespeare's Book: The Story Behind the First Folio and the Making of Shakespeare* reminds us of the obstinacy of what Adam Hooks has called "Folio as fetish" (2016, 185). Laoutaris's title alone contains two tropes that seem to resurface unbidden during Shakespearean centenaries—namely, the ideas that the First Folio somehow *made* (or gave us) Shakespeare and that the First Folio is "Shakespeare's book." (Laoutaris finds "enticing" evidence for the involvement in the Folio's publication of Shakespeare's London lodger, a man of murky identity who may have acted on the deceased Shakespeare's behalf; Shakespeare has long provided fertile ground for speculative histories [341].) But if the First Folio can be said to be Shakespeare's, it has become so only posthumously and by way of wishful thinking and mere assertion. As Adam Hooks writes, "The Folio does not give us Shakespeare. Rather, it gives us a particular version of Shakespeare"—one among many, Hooks implies (2016, 185). Comparatively underexamined, the later Folios offer up fresh and ample quarry for bibliographical work. The number of extant copies of the later Folios (as recorded in the online *Shakespeare Census*; see Zachary Lesser's chapter in this volume) gives some sense of the variety and scale of the evidence that awaits analysis: some 182 copies of the Third Folio, 373 copies of the Second, and 339 copies of the Fourth are known to survive (the *Census* adds to these figures several dozen Folio fragments). In this trove there are no doubt discoveries to be made.

This should not suggest that the later Folios have gone unexamined. Far from it; scholars have considered the progress of Shakespeare in print *after* the First Folio with far-reaching implications for our understanding of the reception and evolution of the Shakespeare canon (see, for instance, Sonia Massai's *Shakespeare and the Rise of the Editor* [2007], which found evidence of editorial work being done in the Fourth Folio; Eric Rasmussen's ongoing investigations into the Fourth Folio's printing history [1998, 2017]; and Emma Depledge and Peter Kirwan's volume *Canonising Shakespeare: Stationers and the Book Trade, 1640–1740* [2017], which conspicuously excludes the First Folio from its ambit). But against the exhaustive and often repetitious work done on the First Folio, the later Folios are relative enigmas. And as bibliographical scholarship turns away from textual authority and the priority of editions and toward more discursive, contingent, and embodied topics and kinds of evidence (bindings, marginal annotations, histories of book use and reception), we are well positioned to consider the later folios and the stories they tell. This book seeks to move in that direction.

The chapters in this book reflect the themes and preoccupations of two exhibitions held to mark the quatercentenary (1623–2023) of the First Folio. Organized in collaboration with Pittsburgh's Frick Art Museum by Carnegie Mellon University (CMU) Libraries, these exhibits ran concurrently in two venues. One exhibit, *Inventing Shakespeare: Text, Technology, and the Four Folios*, was installed in the Hunt Library at Carnegie Mellon University, and the other, *From Stage to Page: 400 Years of Shakespeare in Print*, was installed in the Frick's Jacobean Gallery—an octagonal room paneled in seventeenth-century oak that evoked the Folios' cultural and historical origins. Spare by design, *From Stage to Page* spotlighted all seven Shakespeare Folios held in CMU Libraries' Special Collections: one copy of the First, and two copies each of the Second, Third, and

Fourth Folios. *From Stage to Page* represented an unusual (and, in Pittsburgh, unprecedented) opportunity to view the First Folio alongside copies of each of the later Folios—it was also the first time that all seven Shakespeare Folios held at Carnegie Mellon were put on public display. Beyond exhibiting the richness of CMU Libraries' holdings in early Shakespeare editions, *From Stage to Page* offered a synoptic view of how the four Folios brought about Shakespeare's literary canonization in the seventeenth century. The second exhibit, *Inventing Shakespeare*, illustrated the ways in which the Folios have prompted new and inventive methods for research. Rightly called "the most thoroughly studied early modern book," the First Folio has inspired an array of scholarly tools, techniques, and technologies (Galbraith 2010, 46). From Charlton Hinman's optical-mechanical collating machine (a functioning example of which is held in CMU's Special Collections [fig. 6.4]), to the *Shakespeare Virtual Reality (VR)* project (https://shakespeare-vr.library.cmu.edu/), to digital and photographic facsimiles, to ongoing experiments in bibliographical analysis using computer vision and machine learning, *Inventing Shakespeare* ranged widely.

Though designed to accompany and augment these exhibits, this book is not an exhibition catalog. Instead, its essay-chapters reflect the viewpoints and research of their authors, many of whom have written widely elsewhere on the subject of Shakespeare's plays in print. Whenever possible, however, the illustrations in this book are sourced from the Carnegie Mellon University copies of the four Shakespeare Folios, offering a virtual display of the seven Carnegie Mellon Folios and a scholarly addendum to both 2023 exhibitions, if not a word-for-word reprinting of their wall text and labels.

What unites the chapters in this book is their interest in how the First Folio evolved through the Second, Third, and Fourth. Far from being mere lossy imitations of the First Folio, the three later Folios offer up fascinating idiosyncrasies, some of which have only recently been studied or fully noted. The Third Folio, for instance, exists in two forms. One, dated 1663 on its title page, is an otherwise untroubled reprint of the Second Folio (1632), which preceded it by three decades. The second form (properly an "issue") of the Third Folio, however, bears a 1664 date on its reprinted title page and contains seven plays (six apocryphal) that do not appear in either the First or Second Folios. Surviving copies of the Third Folio therefore represent two distinct issues, each marked by the presence or absence of the seven plays that the 1664 title page loudly trumpets as "never before Printed in Folio." CMU Special Collections holds one copy of each issue (fig. i.1). The reason for the Third Folio's reissue is believed to have been commercial rather than literary: its booksellers sought a way to differentiate the Third Folio from both the Second and First, making it more salable (see Tara Lyons's chapter).

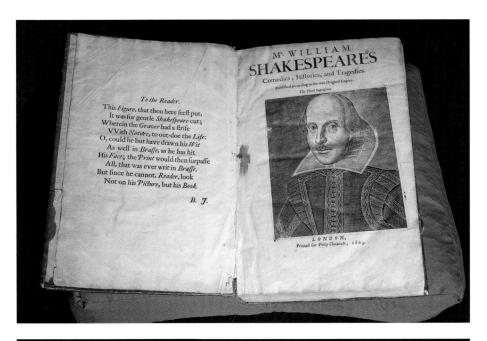

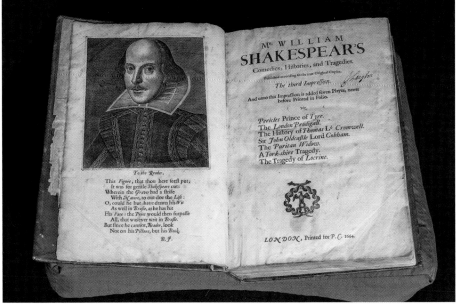

FIGURE I.I The two states of the Third Folio's title page, distinguishing the 1663 and 1664 issues. Carnegie Mellon University Libraries, Special Collections, PR2751 .A4 1663 (*top*) and Posner PR2751 .A4 1664 (*bottom*).

The Fourth Folio, printed in 1685, embraces oddities of its own. Seventeen of its sheets (a full sixty-eight pages) were reprinted as late as 1700—fifteen years after the edition's first appearance. The reasons for the reprinting of these seventeen sheets remain obscure. Scholars (Dawson 1952; Hansen and Rasmussen 2017) have suggested that the printer of the deficient 1685 sheets failed to deliver the required quantity, leaving the bookseller who inherited the unsold copies short-sheeted. The missing sheets may also have been damaged—torn, sodden, soiled—or simply lost while in the bookseller's warehouse and thus required replacement. Giles Dawson (1952) proposed that copies of the Fourth Folio that contain these reprinted sheets "constitute a fifth folio," different enough in kind to earn their own classification. What's more, the identities of the Fourth Folio's printers have long been unknown, making the circumstances of its publication and printing more enigmatic than those of the First (see the chapter by Lemley et al. in this volume). The Fourth Folio also contains one of the most glaring typesetting errors in the history of English literature: the printed subtitle for Hamlet reads, "RPINCE OF DENMARK" (fig. 6.1).

The texts of Shakespeare's plays in all four Folios offer up other, "literal" variants besides: these are errors introduced in the process of printing and range from inverted or damaged pieces of type to the omission or alteration of entire lines of dialogue. Such misprints were corrected occasionally during presswork—provided, of course they were noticed during proofreading. Offending pieces of type were removed and replaced while the page bearing the error was at press. These tardy interventions mean that copies containing sheets with corrections make up new, recognizable "states" of the text. These many hundreds of small aberrations are masked behind the nominal tidiness of the word "copy." In truth, no two copies of any of the four Folios are known to be exactly alike—each copy differs in some way from the next. The definite article is thus misplaced: there is no "the" First Folio. Rather, each of the four Folios is plural, every copy conveying a subtly unique form of Shakespeare's plays—yet another reason to prefer a composite or multiple view of the Folios.

Beyond variants introduced by way of the proofreader's correcting pen, there are also variants at the level of individual copies introduced by the Folios' earliest readers and owners: inscriptions, marginal annotations, sketches made by children, or bits of bookkeeping or arithmetic made in the margin. These traces of a book's provenance (what William Sherman has likened to a fossil record of a bookish "ecology of use and reuse" [Sherman 2010, 6]) offer up poignant clues of the many lives that books live (see Zachary Lesser's chapter). One of the copies of the Fourth Folio at Carnegie Mellon University, for instance, hints at its origins at Belton House, the Lincolnshire estate of the Brownlowe family. On one of the book's front flyleaves appears a pair of inscribed names: Alice and

8 | THE FOUR SHAKESPEARE FOLIOS

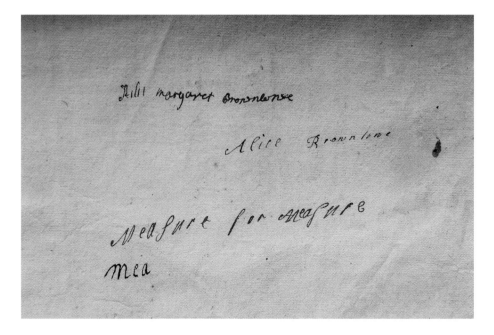

FIGURE I.2 The inscribed names of Alice and Margaret Brownlowe, the earliest documented users of this copy of the Fourth Folio. Carnegie Mellon University Libraries, Special Collections, PR2751 .A4 1685.

Margaret Brownlowe (fig. i.2). We can be reasonably confident that "Alice" is Alice Brownlowe, wife of John Brownlowe, who undertook a campaign of renovation at Belton House in the 1680s and funded the expansion of its library (including, presumably, the acquisition of the Fourth Folio) in the same period. The second name is more obscure: it appears that the writer began inscribing "Alice" in a style that imitates the other, complete inscription. Changing tack, however, the writer instead spelled out her own name in full: Margaret Brownlowe. What stories can this pair of names tell? Is this evidence of the elder Alice teaching her daughter Margaret (1687–1710) to spell her name? The Shakespearean play title written out below the two names, *Measure for Measure*, suggests as much: a less confident hand has attempted to copy out the title, giving up three letters in. Or perhaps it's another daughter, also Alice (or Alicia) (1684–1727), named after her mother, conspiring with her sister to mark the Folio's blank leaves with their names? In either case, these inscriptions show that Shakespeare Folios functioned as objects of familial and matrilineal recordkeeping; they also suggest that John Brownlowe was this copy's first owner, though his daughters were, it seems, its earliest users. A portrait that survives at Belton House shows Margaret at eight years old, allowing us to put a face to at least one of these haltingly inscribed names (even while the identity of the Black child attending her in the portrait remains unknown) (fig. i.3).

FIGURE 1.3   Henry Tilson, portrait of Margaret Brownlowe (1687–1710), aged eight, 1695. The National Trust, 986143, Belton House. © National Trust Images.

The bindings of the Folios also vary, telling stories of their own. Before the introduction of edition binding—a method by which every copy of a particular print run is bound up in the same or similar style—books were kept in sheets or only loosely-stitched together until they were sold. The buyer then had the sheets bound in a style of their choosing. Both of CMU's copies of the Third Folio are in their original bindings, exhibiting a strikingly similar style: plain calf with a double line of embossed rules outlining the edge of each board and a mottled pattern of red decorating the edges of the text block. Separated for nearly four centuries, both of these books—perhaps bound in the same workshop in London with the same tools and from the same stock of materials (animal hide, paper, twine, pigment, and glue)—have been reunited by chance in Pittsburgh.

While this book does not address all of these topics, its chapters find common ground in considering how the four Folios relate and diverge. Andrew Murphy's chapter outlines the often circuitous paths by which the rights to print Shakespeare's plays traded hands in the seventeenth century. Before copyright, rights in individual titles were registered and held by printers, stationers, or booksellers and not—as is usually the case today—by their authors. As a result, each Folio emerged from protracted and often contentious negotiations between the many rights-holders of Shakespeare's plays. That a consortium of these rights-holders came to terms at all is in some ways miraculous: as Murphy's chapter makes clear, the First Folio and the three Folios that followed all owe their existence to these ad hoc collaborative networks.

Claire M. L. Bourne's chapter turns to the material conditions of the Folios' making. Offering an account of the First Folio's design and typography, Bourne shows that Shakespeare's legacy in print owes much to the labor and homespun materials of the early modern print shop: type, ink, paper. Though Bourne focuses primarily on the First Folio, she ends by observing that the material histories of all four Folios are more alike than dissimilar: the resemblances among the four Folios—typographic, material, formal—register a continuity of Shakespeare in print (and in folio) across the seventeenth century.

Erin Blake's chapter examines what is probably the most recognizable feature of the Folios—the engraved portrait of Shakespeare. Describing and discerning the states in which the engraving survives, Blake argues that its placement directly on the First Folio's title page represented a startling departure from the norm. Summarizing current knowledge on the subject, Blake also disentangles the identity of the portrait's engraver, Martin Droeshout.

Tara Lyons's chapter considers the cultural and economic status of folios in the period. The folio format, Lyons reminds us, was not just a sign of literary ambition but could also represent a pragmatic choice made to cut costs and persuade would-be buyers. Affording a higher word-to-page ratio than smaller formats, printing in folio allowed the Folios' backers to profitably issue all of Shakespeare's plays in volumes of increasing size (the Fourth, as Lyons points out, is the largest of the four Folios).

The chapters by Zachary Lesser and Samuel Lemley et al., meanwhile, mark a thematic turn. Both consider recent technological interventions in the study of the Folios. Lesser's chapter draws on data gathered in the *Shakespeare Census* (https://shakespearecensus.org/) to account for the often unpredictable ways in which copies of the Folios changed hands, crossed borders, and accrued evidence of use. The chapter by Lemley et al. draws on computational bibliography as a new species of analysis of early printed books—one that uses computer vision and machine learning to detect bibliographical evidence. Deploying these computational tools on the Fourth Folio, Lemley et al. reveal who printed (and reprinted) it in 1685 and 1700. If the first four chapters study the four Folios' publication and printing in the seventeenth century, these final two chapters study the Folios' afterlives—from the viewpoint of provenance, institutional history, and connoisseurship, and from the viewpoint of scholarly method, respectively.

In a way, this volume takes the form of a bibliographical anatomy. Each chapter examines some aspect or constituent part of the four Folios, explaining the collection's subtitle: *Copy, Print, Paper, Type*. Lesser attends quantitatively to the survival and afterlives of individual copies, Bourne to the materiality and typography of the First and later Folios, Lyons to the cultural work of folios in the period, Blake to the engraved print of Shakespeare's face, and Murphy to the commercial and professional mechanisms—the evolving ownership of "copy"— that brought the four Folios to a paying public. In its piecewise scrutiny of the Folios, the book adopts a metaphor that appears in the First Folio's prefatory "Address to the Readers," written by the Folio's editors. In the Address, Heminge and Condell write that the Folio presents Shakespeare's plays, "cured, and perfect of their limbs," an image that suggests the posthumous care of Shakespeare's literary body. In attempting to reconcile and join the Four Folios into a shared narrative—to cure and perfect points of disjunction between them—this book and the exhibitions it accompanies linger over several aspects of Shakespeare's plays in folio, either material or cultural. Some chapters narrow in on the particular (Blake's chapter finds meaning in a single engraved line, made to represent a strand of Shakespeare's hair), while others revel in the aggregate (Lesser's writing depends on data points gathered from hundreds of copies of each of the Folios, while Lemley et al. sift tens of thousands of distinctively damaged pieces of seventeenth-century type). Collectively, though, the book's chapter-essays offer an account of the four Shakespeare Folios that is accessible, lively, coherent, and authoritative. They provide, if not a complete account of the four Shakespeare Folios, a number of inventive forays into their makeup and meaning.

CHAPTER 1

Publishing the Four Folios

Andrew Murphy

In 1576, when Shakespeare was twelve years old, the Theatre in Shoreditch opened for business. It was likely the first venue in England to stage professional plays and charge spectators an entrance fee to see them. When Shakespeare, as an adult, arrived in London some years later, and began acting in and writing plays, he was thus joining what was, in effect, still quite a new sector of the entertainment business. In its earliest years, the theater could sometimes be a rather unstable institution. It was, for instance, often disrupted in times when the plague was particularly virulent in London, with the entire theater sector sometimes being shut down in an effort to help contain the spread of the disease. On such occasions, those who worked in the theater had to find other ways of making a living. During one extended period of closure, in 1592–93, Shakespeare himself turned to writing narrative poetry, bringing the text of *Venus and Adonis* to the London printer and publisher (and fellow Stratfordian) Richard Field, in the hope of making some money by selling the text for publication. A second narrative poem, *The Rape of Lucrece*, appeared in the following year. Soon enough, however, the doors of the theaters reopened, and Shakespeare was back to his routine business of writing plays, with poetry for its own sake becoming, it seems, a less immediate interest.

Both *Venus and Adonis* and *The Rape of Lucrece* were successful texts, appearing in numerous editions over the course of the following decades and turning a healthy profit for the publishers who issued them. We may wonder whether, when Shakespeare ventured down to Field's shop, he might have speculated as to whether there might also be a publishing market for his playscripts. By contrast with his poems, these texts were not, in fact, Shakespeare's to sell, since plays were the property of the theater companies who commissioned them. But if he did indeed ponder the issue of the market potential of his plays, Shakespeare might, as a frequenter of London bookshops, have registered that—at least in the early years of the theater—the major London publishers had seemed slow enough to take an interest in plays from the commercial playhouses (Lesser 2011). Perhaps, he might have concluded, they may, to begin with, have hesitated over whether the general public would have much enthusiasm for stage performances reproduced in flat, unlively print.

Whatever the playwright's own thoughts—if any—might have been on the matter, in the very next year after Field published *Venus and Adonis*, one publisher did take a chance on bringing Shakespeare's plays to print. This was Thomas Millington, who was, in every sense, a peripheral figure: a small-scale operator, whose business was located at the top of Cornhill in London, some little distance from the center of the publishing trade in St. Paul's Churchyard. Millington issued editions of *2 Henry VI* and *Titus Andronicus* in 1594, with *3 Henry VI* following in the next year. His speculative venture paid off, with new editions of his *Henry*s appearing in 1600, a likely sign that the original editions had sold out (or were close to selling out) by then. In the same year, Millington also issued an edition of *Henry V*, and Edward White issued a second edition of *Titus*. In the wake of the first appearance of Millington's texts, a number of other publishers followed him into the Shakespeare market. The history plays proved notably popular and accounted for a little over 50 percent of the total pool of his texts published during Shakespeare's own lifetime (Lyons 2012). Beyond the history plays, *Romeo and Juliet* and *Hamlet* both appeared in three editions in this period, and a range of other texts were also issued in single editions.

By the time of Shakespeare's death in 1616, roughly half of his plays had made their way into print. In the final stretch of his life, however, the publishing record became a little patchy. In 1610, no plays by Shakespeare were brought to print. In 1611, editions of *Hamlet*, *Pericles*, and *Titus Andronicus* were published, but this would be the only time in this period in which more than one play appeared in a single year. The years 1612 and 1613 each saw the publication of just one play, drawn from the reliable canon of the history plays: *Richard III* and *1 Henry IV*, respectively. There were, again, no texts published in 1614, and in 1615, once more, a single history play, *Richard II*, was published. When Shakespeare died in 1616, no play of his was brought to print, nor were any plays published in the two years following.

In the period immediately after Shakespeare's death, the publication of his works can be said to have arrived at something of a crossroads. Had the pattern we have just logged endured, then it might well have been the case that the publishing of his plays would have continued in a sporadic fashion, being increasingly restricted to editions of the tried and trusted history plays—a process that might have been given further impetus by the fact that, while Shakespeare's texts remained part of his company's repertoire, they were also increasingly competing for stage time with the work of younger, more modish playwrights. If this had happened, then Shakespeare would, in the long term, have ended up being a much-diminished literary figure, best known for a small handful of solidly popular historical plays, supplemented by an attenuated canon of texts less frequently reprinted. However, in 1619, something a little unexpected happened. That year witnessed the largest release of Shakespeare plays (including two plays misattributed to him) ever to have been issued in a single year: a total of ten texts. The publisher behind this set of editions was Thomas Pavier, and he worked in collaboration with the printer William Jaggard. The history of their project is complex, but a fundamental point to be made in relation to it here is that it effectively helped to set a new direction for Shakespeare publishing (Lesser 2021). Precisely what Pavier and Jaggard were essaying in issuing their collection of texts is uncertain, but it seems clear that they had some notion of offering the public a set of plays that could be thought of as potentially constituting a collection. The individual plays could be purchased separately, but several instances have been identified of all of the plays being acquired together, and then being bound into a single volume. Pavier and Jaggard therefore seem to have been the first members of the publishing trade to have explored the idea of offering the public something greater than individual Shakespeare titles issued largely in isolation from each other.

Just four years after the appearance of the 1619 texts, the Jaggard firm found itself putting another Shakespeare collection through its print shop. Whether by conscious intent or not, the 1619 venture had effectively served as a kind of test bed for this new enterprise. Firstly, it helped to demonstrate that there actually still was a viable market for Shakespeare's plays, and that interest in the texts extended beyond the histories, as, in addition to *2* and *3 Henry VI* and *Henry V*, the Pavier-Jaggard set included *The Merry Wives of Windsor, A Midsummer Night's Dream, The Merchant of Venice, King Lear,* and *Pericles.* The project further established that there appeared to be an appetite among at least some book buyers specifically for purchasing a *set* of Shakespeare texts as a single entity. Beyond this, the venture can also be said to have drawn attention to an important practical issue. The 1619 texts were printed in quarto format, which was the established standard size for individual plays. But binding the whole set together produced a thick and rather ungainly volume. Where Pavier and Jaggard had included ten texts in their collection, a total of eighteen individual titles had been printed over the course of Shakespeare's lifetime. If a new collection were to include all of these texts—and, indeed, potentially to add further plays that had not previously appeared in print—then the quarto format would have been impractical, as it would have produced an unfeasibly unwieldy book. For this reason, the new collection was produced in the larger folio format, as the folio-sized volume offered roughly twice the page area of its quarto counterpart, thereby significantly increasing the amount of text that could be included on each page. The larger page also allowed for a two-columned layout, further maximizing the use of space.

Undertaking the Folio edition was an expensive proposition. It has been estimated that the cost of the paper alone would have run to nearly £100 (Taylor et al. 2016, lxiii). To put this into perspective: a skilled tradesman in London would have had to work for more than two whole years to earn this amount of money (Boulton 1996). It is not clear exactly who initiated the Folio scheme, but one of the primary figures involved was the publisher Edward Blount, who worked closely in conjunction with the Jaggard firm as the project's printer (Higgins 2022). It is likely that Blount was the one who would have provided a significant proportion of the capital needed to set the project in motion. By contrast with the first publisher of Shakespeare's plays, Thomas Millington, Blount was a well-established figure within the trade, with premises at the Black Bear, in the heart of St. Paul's Churchyard. He had served his apprenticeship under William Ponsonby, the foremost literary publisher of the later decades of the sixteenth century. Ponsonby issued editions of the work of Edmund Spenser, Philip Sidney, and other important English authors. Blount concluded his ten-year apprenticeship with Ponsonby in 1588, and, opening up his own business, he followed in his master's footsteps, publishing work by Christopher Marlowe, Ben Jonson, Samuel Daniel, and others. His literary tastes extended beyond the narrowly English, as he also published translations of work by authors such as Montaigne and Cervantes, as well as an Italian dictionary compiled by John Florio and a Spanish grammar written by Cæsar Oudin.

In establishing the Shakespeare project, Blount would have worked closely with Shakespeare's theater company, the King's Men. It seems likely that it was through this connection that Blount was able to gain access to those texts of Shakespeare that had never previously been published. In November 1623, Blount and Isaac Jaggard (William Jaggard's son) registered ownership of sixteen such texts with the Stationers' Company, thus almost doubling the canon as it had previously appeared in print. For those plays that had already been published, a

FIGURE 1.1 The colophon included at the end of the First Folio, indicating both the venture's senior partners (Jaggard and Blount) and the junior partners (Smethwick—his name in a variant spelling here—and Aspley). Carnegie Mellon University Libraries, Special Collections, PR2751 .A4 1623.

series of (sometimes complex) negotiations were required in order to secure the right to reproduce the plays in the new edition. Some of the other rights-holders were drawn into the scheme as junior partners, and thus the credit line at the end of the volume indicates that it was "printed at the charges of W. Jaggard, Ed. Blount, I. Smithweeke and W. Aspley" (fig. 1.1). "I. Smithweeke" was John Smethwick, who held the rights to *Hamlet*, *Romeo and Juliet*, *Love's Labour's Lost*, and *The Taming of a Shrew* (a play different from, but related to, *The Taming of the Shrew*—but ownership of the rights to *A Shrew* would likely have given Smethwick a claim on the rights to *The Shrew*). William Aspley had published editions of *2 Henry IV* and *Much Ado About Nothing* in 1600, in partnership with Andrew Wise. He had also previously copublished books with Blount, and their business premises were two doors down from each other in the Churchyard, so the partnership arrangement would probably have made obvious sense to the two men (Blayney 1990, 3).

As we have seen, the adoption of the folio format was a matter of necessity, given the sheer quantity of text that needed to be included in the volume. However, as the folio was the largest standard book size, the format also traditionally signaled a certain element of prestige. The Shakespeare Folio played a little on this notion by including a rather elaborate set of preliminaries in the volume: a title-page image of Shakespeare; a poem on the facing page by one of his best-known fellow playwrights, Ben Jonson; further celebratory poems by other noted writers of the day; an extended declaration dedicating the volume to the Earls of Pembroke and Montgomery; and an address "to the great Variety of Readers." The last two texts mentioned here were both signed by John Heminges and Henry Condell. Both these men were members of the King's Men company, and they were, in fact, the only remaining survivors of the original group from which it had evolved, the Lord Chamberlain's Men. They had thus been among Shakespeare's closest colleagues over an extended period. The connections between the three men went deeper than this, however, as, during Shakespeare's time as a lodger in Silver Street in London, Heminges and Condell and their families had been close neighbors. That the professional relationship extended to personal friendship is indicated by the fact that Shakespeare, in his will, left a gold coin to each of them to buy a ring to mark his memory.

While Heminges and Condell were both actors, Heminges actually also had a strong business background. He had served an apprenticeship in the Grocers' Company, being made free of the Company in 1587. Given this experience and expertise, it is likely that Heminges would have been a primary company-side point of contact for the Folio as a commercial venture and that he would have been keen to ensure that the publication was a financial success. We certainly see a business-driven imperative at play in the address "to the Great Variety of Readers," which—while it offers high praise to Heminges and Condell's late colleague, styling him "a happie imitator of Nature . . . a most gentle expresser of it" whose "mind and hand went together"—also persistently urges the casual bookshop browser to purchase the volume: "Read . . . but buy it first . . . what euer you do, Buy." This is, indeed, we might say, a hard sell of quite a high order.

Heminges and Condell's "Great Variety of Readers" are envisaged as numbering "from the most able, to him that can but spell." In this sense, the imagined readership for the book is very wide indeed, ranging from fluent readers to those who are barely literate. In practice, however, the number of those who could have purchased the volume was likely to have been quite restricted. A bound copy of the book probably cost about £1 (Blayney 1991, 25–26). While it is extremely hard to equate this price to a contemporary equivalent, if we again use the measure of the pay rate of a skilled London tradesman, we can say that it would have taken about nine days' wages at that rate to earn enough money to buy a copy of the book. It comes as no surprise, then, to discover that most of the early purchase records tend to relate to copies acquired by aristocratic or other well-off households (Mayer 2018).

For those who *could* afford the volume, what exactly did they find between its covers? Here we discover a strong contrast between the Pavier-Jaggard venture and its folio successor. The 1619 collection offered a rather miscellaneous set of texts, mixing together different kinds of plays and including two texts that have generally not been accepted into the canon. Some of the plays also appeared in the collection in significantly abridged, sometimes slightly garbled versions. The Folio project, by contrast, offered full texts of all plays, with every one having clear canonical credentials. The Folio also aimed to present a collection that was ordered and orderly. The plays were distributed into three generic categories: comedies, histories, and tragedies, and the middle group here offered a very particular definition of what constituted history. As Tara L. Lyons has noted, this category was reserved for plays about English kings who reigned after the Norman conquest (Lyons 2012, 205). Macbeth, Cymbeline, Lear, and the Romans had to find lodging elsewhere (with the tragedies). This generic division of the plays shaped—and continues to shape—the way in which they were perceived both individually and in relation to each other. This arrangement is, for instance, one of the reasons why we tend to think of eight of the history plays as being organized into two continuous "tetralogies," conceiving of the plays as offering a linked narrative by reign.

The compilers of the volume also sought to impose a certain amount of order on the plays individually. *The Tempest*—the first play in the volume—is systematically divided into acts and scenes, and it concludes with an indication of the location of the action ("an vn-inhabited Island") and a list of the "Names of the Actors" (not a catalogue of those company members who performed in the play, but rather a record of the different roles in the text, what we would now style a "dramatis personae" list). In this list the characters are ordered broadly by rank, with the result that Alonso, as king, appears in first place, ahead of Prospero. Caliban, though characterized as "a saluage and deformed slaue" is, interestingly, listed ahead of the lower-class comic characters Trinculo and Stephano. The other ordering principle at play is gender, with the result that Miranda appears in fourteenth place, just below the generic "Marriners," though above Ariel, perhaps giving us a sense that this character may have been thought of as female in the original productions (Ariel has, over the centuries, been played both by male and female actors). By the same ordering principle, in *Othello*, Desdemona is listed after the "Saylors" and the "Clowne." The level of systematization we find in *The Tempest* is not, however, carried forward through all of the texts. Few of the other plays include dramatis personae lists, and the act and scene divisions are oftentimes more than a little haphazard. *The Comedy of Errors* is divided into five acts, but, despite the appearance of "*scena prima*" in four of the act headings, the individual scenes in each act are not actually marked. While *Love's Labour's Lost* marks five acts, two of them are headed "*Actus Quartus*." In

Henry V, the appearance of the Chorus is generally taken as signaling the beginning of each new act, but whoever divided the play in the First Folio missed the entry of the Chorus at the start of the second act, with the result that act three is misidentified as act two, act four as act three, and an incorrect act four marker is introduced immediately before Fluellen's "Kill the poyes and the luggage." Most striking of all, perhaps, is the fact that the entirety of *Antony and Cleopatra* is designated *"Actus Primus. Scæna Prima."*

Though the Folio's attempts to systematize the text of the plays are inconsistent across the volume, nevertheless, they did serve to establish a broad set of principles that would increasingly be brought into play in later periods, when successive editors from the eighteenth century onwards applied the same rules to the text in a more consistent and methodical fashion. Indeed, the principle of ordering characters by gender would persist well into the twentieth century. Thus, for instance, in a 1955 edition of *Romeo and Juliet*, edited by John Dover Wilson, Juliet is listed in twenty-second place in the dramatis personae list, as Wilson was following strictly a combination of the social status and gender rules that we find in the First Folio.

We do not know exactly how many copies of the Folio were printed, but one estimate is that the likeliest figure may have been 750 (Blayney 1991, 2). Of these, in excess of two hundred have survived, meaning that, in the strictest sense of the term, the Folio is not a "rare" book (Rasmussen et al. 2012; Hooks and Lesser n.d.). In its own time, it seems likely that, despite its cost, the volume must have sold reasonably well, since a new edition appeared in 1632, just nine years after the first edition. By the time the new edition appeared, many of those involved in the original project had died. William Jaggard died in the year that the first edition appeared, and his son Isaac—who had taken over the project from his ailing father as it progressed through the family print shop—died just four years later. In the same year, Henry Condell died and he was followed by John Heminges in 1630. One of the volume's dedicatees, William Herbert, the Earl of Pembroke, died in the same year as Heminges. Edward Blount, the primary publisher, survived into the year that the Second Folio edition appeared. Throughout the 1620s, however, his business had progressively been failing, and by 1627 he had given up the Black Bear.

Though so many of those involved in the First Folio did not live to see it run to a second edition, there were still some continuities between the two volumes. John Smethwick and William Aspley both survived to serve once again as, essentially, junior publishing partners in the new venture. We also find some continuities in the Black Bear premises. The publisher who had taken over the business from Edward Blount in 1627 was Robert Allott. Allott had become a freeman of the Stationers' Company in 1625 and, in the following year, he published a text by Lewis Bayly entitled *The Practice of Piety*, with Isaac Jaggard serving as printer (McKerrow 1910). Allott quickly found that he had a bestseller on his hands, as he issued fourteen editions of the work over a period of ten years. In 1629, he published a Welsh translation of the text, which appeared in a second edition under his imprint in the immediately following year. While Allott published many other texts as well—including editions of Philip Massinger's plays *The Roman Actor* and *The Maid of Honour*, and Ben Jonson's *Bartholomew Fair*—it seems likely that Bayly's religious volume was a central text helping to drive the commercial success of his business, being a steady, reliable seller year after year. Certainly, by 1630, he had built up enough financial resources that he was able to purchase Blount's rights in Shakespeare. Thus the Black Bear came to serve, once again, as a central location for a Shakespeare folio venture.

As we have already noted, Isaac Jaggard died in 1627—the year after he published *The Practice of Piety* for Allott. His business was taken over by one of his father's former apprentices, Thomas Cotes, who had gained his freedom from the Stationers' Company in 1606 (Plomer 1907). In addition to acquiring the Jaggard printing business, Cotes (in conjunction with his brother Richard) also acquired the Jaggard portion to the central tranche of Shakespeare rights. In the very year that he took over the Jaggard premises, Cotes made a connection with Allott, as he served as printer for another new edition of Bayly's *Practice of Piety*. Once Allott acquired the other half of the Jaggard-Blount Shakespeare rights, it made sense for him to enter into a partnership with the Cotes brothers, which essentially replicated the relationship between Edward Blount and William Jaggard and his son—the men combining to serve as the primary agents taking forward a new Shakespeare Folio project. Two other publishers were brought into the venture: Richard Hawkins and Richard Meighen, who had, in the years following the appearance of the First Folio, acquired the rights to, respectively, *Othello* and *The Merry Wives of Windsor*. While all copies of the Second Folio credit the entire group of publishers at the end of the book, a variety of different title pages were issued, each with the name of a different member of the publishing syndicate. Thus, for instance, one state of the Second Folio's imprint credits John Smethwick as publisher, listing his shop in St. Dunstan's Churchyard as the location where the book could be purchased, while the other credits Robert Allot, listing Allot's shop at the Black Bear in St. Paul's Churchyard (figs. 1.2, 1.3).

The continuities between the First and Second Folios extended to the text itself. The Second Folio was, essentially, a page-for-page reprint of its predecessor and the general appearance of the two volumes is very similar—both editions were, after all, produced in the same print shop, using the same type stock and

FIGURE 1.2 When the Second Folio was published, individual title pages were created for the different partners in the venture. In this instance, John Smethwick is credited here as publisher. Carnegie Mellon University Libraries, Special Collections, PR2751 .A4 1632.

FIGURE 1.3 In this copy of the Second Folio, Robert Allot—the primary publisher of the venture—is credited on the title page. Carnegie Mellon University Libraries, Special Collections, PR2751 .A4 1632.

ornaments. The Second Folio compositors sometimes even used the same ornaments in the same positions in the new volume, though they sometimes tended to flip the orientation of the ornaments. A nice example of this can be seen on the opening page of *Much Ado About Nothing* (figs. 1.4, 1.5). Despite following the First Folio page-by-page, the Second Folio compositors sometimes picked up errors in the original and corrected them. Thus, for instance, in the First Folio the final two pages of *The Two Gentlemen of Verona* mistakenly carry the heading "*The Merry Wiues of Windsor*" (the next play in the volume) and the Second Folio compositors correct this. In other instances, however, the Second Folio reproduces errors from the First. In the histories section of both books, for instance, we find a set of page numbers running 88, 91, 92, 91, 92, 93. Likewise, in both editions *2 Henry IV* ends on page 100, to be followed by *Henry V* starting on page 69, with the numbering running forward from there. Beyond the business of the setting of the type, we can say that whoever had prepared the text for printing adopted a fairly active interventionist approach, correcting errors where they were spotted, adjusting the meter in places and restoring many classical names that had become jumbled in the original (Black and Shaaber 1937). Strikingly, for instance, in *Titus Andronicus*, the nonsensical "from *Eptons* rising in the East" is corrected to "from *Hiperions* [i.e., Hyperion's] rising in the East"—an impressive and well-informed feat of unscrambling. For all these intelligent interventions, however, many of the First Folio's errors remained in place: *Love's Labour's Lost* still has two fourth acts, some of the *Henry V* act breaks are still incorrectly located, and *Antony and Cleopatra* continues to be presented as a single act, single scene play.

Where the First Folio edition sold well enough to warrant another edition just nine years after it was issued, the gap to the next folio was significantly longer, running to three decades. By this point, all of the surviving members of the First Folio group had died: William Aspley in 1640, John Smethwick in the following year, and Philip Herbert, the surviving dedicatee of the volume, in 1650. In addition, the entire group who had brought the Second Folio to print had also died: Robert Allott in 1635, Richard Hawkins in 1636 (or 1637), Richard Meighen in 1641 (or 1642), and Thomas Cotes in 1641, followed by Cotes's brother Richard in 1653.

Immediately after Allott died, his widow, Mary Allott, briefly carried on the business in her own right. In 1637, she married Philip Chetwinde, who had been made free of the Clothworkers' Company in 1627 and who remained active in that company throughout his life, becoming Warden in 1654 and Master in 1666 (Dugas 2002). Though he acquired rights to his wife's property on marriage, the fact that he was not a member of the Stationers' Company meant that

Much adoe about Nothing.

Actus primus, Scena prima.

Enter Leonato Gouernour of Messina, Innogen his wife, Hero his daughter, and Beatrice his Neece, with a messenger.

Leonato.

I Learne in this Letter, that *Don Peter* of *Arragon*, comes this night to *Messina*.

Mess. He is very neere by this : he was not three Leagues off when I left him.

Leon. How many Gentlemen haue you lost in this action?

Mess. But few of any sort, and none of name.

Leon. A victorie is twice it selfe, when the atchieuer brings home full numbers : I finde heere, that Don *Peter* hath bestowed much honor on a yong *Florentine*, called *Claudio*.

Mess. Much deseru'd on his part, and equally remembred by Don *Pedro*, he hath borne himselfe beyond the promise of his age, doing in the figure of a Lambe, the feats of a Lion, he hath indeede better bettred expectation, then you must expect of me to tell you how.

Leo. He hath an Vnckle heere in *Messina*, wil be very much glad of it.

Mess. I haue alreadie deliuered him letters, and there appeares much ioy in him, euen so much, that ioy could not shew it selfe modest enough, without a badg of bitternesse.

Leo. Did he breake out into teares?

Mess. In great measure.

Leo. A kinde ouerflow of kindnesse, there are no faces truer, then those that are so wash'd, how much better is it to weepe at ioy, then to ioy at weeping?

Bea. I pray you, is Signior *Mountanto* return'd from the warres, or no?

Mess. I know none of that name, Lady, there was none such in the armie of any sort.

Leon. What is he that you aske for Neece?

Hero. My cousin meanes Signior Benedick of *Padua*.

Mess. O he's return'd, and as pleasant as euer he was.

Beat. He set vp his bils here in *Messina*, & challeng'd Cupid at the Flight : and my Vnckles foole reading the Challenge, subscrib'd for Cupid, and challeng'd him at the Burbolt. I pray you, how many hath hee kil'd and eaten in these warres? But how many hath he kil'd? for indeed, I promis'd to eate all of his killing.

Leon. 'Faith Neece, you taxe Signior Benedicke too much, but hee'l be meet with you, I doubt it not.

Mess. He hath done good seruice Lady in these wars.

Beat. You had musty victuall, and he hath holpe to eate it : he's a very valiant Trencher-man, hee hath an excellent stomacke.

Mess. And a good souldier too Lady.

Beat. And a good souldier to a Lady. But what is he to a Lord?

Mess. A Lord to a Lord, a man to a man, stuft with all honourable vertues.

Beat. It is so indeed, he is no lesse then a stuft man : but for the stuffing well, we are all mortall.

Leon. You must not (sir) mistake my Neece, there is a kind of merry war betwixt Signior Benedick, & her : they neuer meet, but there's a skirmish of wit between them.

Bea. Alas, he gets nothing by that. In our last conflict, foure of his fiue wits went halting off, and now is the whole man gouern'd with one : so that if hee haue wit enough to keepe himselfe warme, let him beare it for a difference betweene himselfe and his horse : For it is all the wealth that he hath lest, to be knowne a reasonable creature. Who is his companion now? He hath euery month a new sworne brother.

Mess. I'st possible?

Beat. Very easily possible : he weares his faith but as the fashion of his hat, it euer changes with ỹ next block.

Mess. I see (Lady) the Gentleman is not in your bookes.

Bea. No, and he were, I would burne my study. But I pray you, who is his companion? Is there no young squarer now, that will make a voyage with him to the diuell?

Mess. He is most in the company of the right noble *Claudio*.

Beat. O Lord, he will hang vpon him like a disease : he is sooner caught then the pestilence, and the taker runs presently mad. God helpe the noble *Claudio*, if hee haue caught the Benedict, it will cost him a thousand pound ere he be cur'd.

Mess. I will hold friends with you Lady.

Bea. Do good friend.

Leo. You'l ne're run mad Neece.

Bea. No, not till a hot Ianuary.

Mess. Don *Pedro* is approach'd.

Enter don Pedro, Claudio, Benedicke, Balthasar, and Iohn the bastard.

Pedro. Good Signior *Leonato*, you are come to meet your trouble : the fashion of the world is to auoid cost, and you encounter it.

Leon. Neuer came trouble to my house in the likenes of your Grace : for trouble being gone, comfort should remaine : but when you depart from me, sorrow abides, and happinesse takes his leaue.

I 3   *Pedro.*

FIGURE 1.4   The opening page of *Much Ado About Nothing* in the First Folio. Note the orientation of the woodblock ornament at the head of the text. Carnegie Mellon University Libraries, Special Collections, PR2751 .A4 1623.

Much adoe about Nothing.

Actus Primus, Scæna Prima.

Enter Leonato Governour of Messina, Innogen his wife, Hero his daughter, and Beatrice his Neece, with a Messenger.

Leonato.
Learne in this Letter, that *Don Peter* of *Arragon* comes this night to *Messina.*

Mess. He is very neere by this : he was not three Leagues off when I left him.

Leon. How many Gentlemen have you lost in this action?

Mess. But few of any sort, and none of name.

Leon. A victory is twice it selfe, when the atchiever brings home full numbers : I find heere, that *Don Peter* hath bestowed much honour on a yong *Florentine*, called *Claudio.*

Mess. Much deserv'd on his part, and equally remembred by Don *Pedro*, he hath borne himselfe beyond the promise of his age, doing in the figure of a Lambe, the feates of a Lyon, he hath indeed better bettred expectation, than you must expect of me to tell you how.

Leo. He hath an Vnckle here in *Messina*, will be very much glad of it.

Mess. I have already delivered him Letters, and there appeares much joy in him, even so much that joy could not shew it selfe modest enough, without a badge of bitternesse.

Leo. Did he breake out into teares?

Mess. In great measure.

Leo. A kinde overflow of kindenesse : there are no faces truer, then those that are so wash'd, how much better is it to weepe at joy, then to joy at weeping?

Bea. I pray you, is Signior *Mountanto* return'd from the warres, or no?

Mess. I know none of that name, Lady, there was none such in the Army of any sort.

Leo. What is he that you aske for Neece?

Hero. My Cousin meanes Signior *Benedicke* of *Padua.*

Mess. O he's return'd, and as pleasant as ever he was.

Beat. He set up his bils heere in *Messina*, and challeng'd Cupid at the Flight : and my Vncles foole reading the Challenge, subscrib'd for Cupid, and Challeng'd him at the Burbolt. I pray you, how many hath hee kill'd and eaten in these warres? But how many hath he kill'd? for indeed, I promis'd to eate all of his killing.

Leon. 'Faith Neece, you taxe Signior *Benedicke* too much, but hee'll be meet with you, I doubt it not.

Mess. He hath done good service Lady in those wars.

Mess. You had musty victuall, and hee hath holpe to eate it : hee's a very valiant Trencher-man, hee hath an excellent stomacke.

Mess. And a good souldier too Lady.

Beat. And a good souldier to a Lady. But what is he to a Lord?

Mess. A Lord to a Lord, a Man to a Man, stuft with all honourable vertues.

Beat. It is so indeed, he is no lesse then a stuft man : but for the stuffing well, we are all mortall.

Leon. You must not (sir) mistake my Neece, there is a kinde of merry War betwixt Signior *Benedicke* and her : they never meet, but there's a skirmish of wit betweene them.

Bea. Alas, he gets nothing by that. In our last conflict, foure of his five wits went halting off, and now is the whole man govern'd with one : so that if hee have wit enough to keepe himselfe warme, let him beare it for a difference betweene himselfe and his horse : For it is all the wealth that he hath left, to be knowne a reasonable creature. Who is his Companion now? He hath every month a new sworne brother.

Mess. I'st possible?

Beat. Very easily possible : he weares his faith but as the fashion of his hat, it ever changes with the next blocke.

Mess. I see (Lady) the Gentleman *is* not in your bookes.

Beat. No, and he were, I would burne my study. But I pray you who is his companion? Is there no young squarer now, that will make a voyage with him to the Divell?

Mess. He is most in the company of the right noble *Claudio.*

Beat. O Lord, he will hang upon him like a disease : he is sooner caught then the Pestilence, and she taker runnes presently madde. God helpe the noble *Claudio*, if he have caught the *Benedicke*, it will cost him a thousand pound ere it be cur'd.

Mess. I will hold friends with you Lady.

Beat. Doe good friend.

Leon. You'll ne're run mad Neece.

Bea. No, not till a hot January.

Mess. Don *Pedro* is approach'd.

Enter Don Pedro, Claudio, Benedicke, Balthazar, and Iohn the bastard.

Pedro. Good Signior *Leonato*, you are come to meete your trouble : the fashion of the world is to avoyd cost, and you encounter it.

Leon. Never came trouble to my house in the likenesse of your Grace : for trouble being gone, comfort should remaine : but when you depart from me, sorrow abides, and happinesse takes his leave.

I 3   *Pedro.*

FIGURE 1.5 The opening page of *Much Ado About Nothing* in the Second Folio. While the same ornament has been used as in the First Folio (see fig. 1.4), here the block has been inverted. Carnegie Mellon University Libraries, Special Collections, PR2751 .A4 1632.

Chetwinde was not immediately entitled to publish the texts that she had inherited. The couple initially attempted to sell the Allott publishing rights and dispose of the Black Bear shop, but in the process Chetwinde became entangled in a complex legal dispute regarding the business, which dragged on for a protracted period (Williams 1977).

By 1654 the legal case concerning the Allott business would seem largely to have run into the sand and Chetwinde began publishing in his own right—apparently without significant opposition from the Stationers' Company. He commenced by issuing a series of editions of Bayly's *Practice of Piety*—the title that had been such a lucrative staple for Robert Allott when he started out as a publisher. Again, like Allott, he also issued a Welsh translation of the text. Chetwinde may have been motivated to think also about the old Allott interest in Shakespeare in the wake of the reopening of the theaters in 1660, which helped to prompt a general revival of interest in the playwright's work (Depledge 2018). By contrast with the Folios of 1623 and 1632, Chetwinde acknowledged no publishing partners in relation to his own volume. A conspicuous absence in the imprint is the name of Ellen Cotes—the widow of Richard Cotes. Like Mary Allott, Ellen Cotes had inherited her husband's business on his death but, unlike Mary, she carried on the business under her own name for an extended period of time and was a printer of some considerable substance. It seems strange that Chetwinde did not enter into the same arrangement with Ellen Cotes that Allott had agreed with her husband and brother-in-law—a relationship that, as we have seen, mirrored that of Edward Blount and William and Isaac Jaggard. Whatever the reason for this might have been, Chetwinde would certainly have had to pay Cotes for the right to publish that segment of the Shakespeare canon for which she still held the rights.

Though different in general appearance and style from the first two Folios, Chetwinde's volume nevertheless followed them page for page in terms of the distribution of the main body of the text. Unlike the first two Folios, the page numbering is continuous throughout the book, and those numbering errors common to both the First and Second Folios in the comedies section have been corrected. Though the Third Folio offers further corrections to the body of the text, some of the errors registered in the first two Folios again persist: *Love's Labour's Lost* continues to have two fourth acts; misplaced act breaks are repeated in *Henry V*; *Antony and Cleopatra* is still a one-act, one-scene play.

In the very next year after it first appeared, Chetwinde reissued his text with a new title page, announcing that "unto this Impression is added seven Playes, never before Printed in Folio" (fig. 1.6). These texts were *Pericles, The London Prodigal, The History of Thomas Lord Cromwell, Sir John Oldcastle, The Puritan*

MR. WILLIAM SHAKESPEAR'S

Comedies, Histories, and Tragedies.

Published according to the true Original Copies.

The third Impression.

And unto this Impression is added seven Playes, never before Printed in Folio.

viz.

Pericles Prince of *Tyre*.
The *London Prodigall*.
The History of *Thomas* Ld. *Cromwell*.
Sir *John Oldcastle* Lord *Cobham*.
The *Puritan Widow*.
A *York-shire* Tragedy.
The Tragedy of *Locrine*.

LONDON, Printed for *P. C.* 1664.

FIGURE 1.6   The title page of the second issue of the Third Folio, listing the "bonus content" that has been added to the text. Carnegie Mellon University Libraries, Special Collections, PR2751 .A4 1664.

Widow, A Yorkshire Tragedy, and *The Tragedy of Locrine.* All of these texts had previously been printed in quarto, with *Pericles, The London Prodigal, Sir John Oldcastle,* and *A Yorkshire Tragedy* all having been attributed explicitly to Shakespeare on their title pages. *Thomas Lord Cromwell, The Puritan Widow,* and *Locrine* had all been identified in the previous editions as being "by W. S." It seems likely that Chetwinde thought of these texts as offering "bonus content" that might revivify a set of plays that were now quite an old property, with their author having been dead for almost a half century by this point. It is possible that his attention may have been drawn to the existence of the plays if he had seen a copy of a short text entitled *Tom Tyler and his Wife,* which was published by Francis Kirkman in 1661. Kirkman included at the end of the text a catalogue of plays, with the authors' names being provided. He attributed all of this set of plays explicitly to Shakespeare, with the exception of *Locrine,* which he registered as being by "W. S." (Anonymous 1661). The second issue of Chetwinde's edition had the effect of incorporating these texts into the canon, where they have, ever since, formed the core of the "Shakespeare apocrypha," with their provenance being much debated over the centuries. Only *Pericles* has generally been accepted as having been substantially written by Shakespeare (Sharpe 2012; Kirwan 2015).

In the wake of the appearance of the Third Folio, Chetwinde remained active as a publisher, but he concentrated more and more on issuing editions of the ever-reliable *Practice of Piety*—just over fifty percent of his total output in the years between 1664 and 1680 (the year in which his name appeared on a title page for the last time) is made up of editions of this single title. While his interest in Shakespeare seems not to have been sustained beyond issuing the Third Folio, other publishers did turn their attention to the playwright's work. A notable figure in this regard was Henry Herringman, who was active in the trade for about forty years, starting in 1653. Herringman was the bookseller of choice for the diarist Samuel Pepys and in his diary, Pepys notes, in an entry for June 22, 1668, that he had gone to see a new play called *Evening's Love,* by John Dryden but did "not like it, it being very smutty." Pepys then calls in on Herringman and he reports that the publisher told him that "Dryden doth himself call it but a fifth-rate play" (Pepys 1976, 247, 248). Herringman would have been in a position to know what Dryden thought as he published his work on a regular basis. Drama, in fact, became something of a specialism of Herringman's and he also issued editions of work by Thomas Middleton, Ben Jonson and Beaumont and Fletcher, as well as more contemporary dramatists such as George Etherege, Thomas Shadwell, and William Wycherley.

FIGURE 1.7   In this opening of the Fourth Folio we can see that instead of starting each play on a separate page (as the previous Folios had done), the printer has run one play immediately after the previous text, creating a rather inelegant *mise-en-page*. Carnegie Mellon University Libraries, Special Collections, PR2751 .A4 1685.

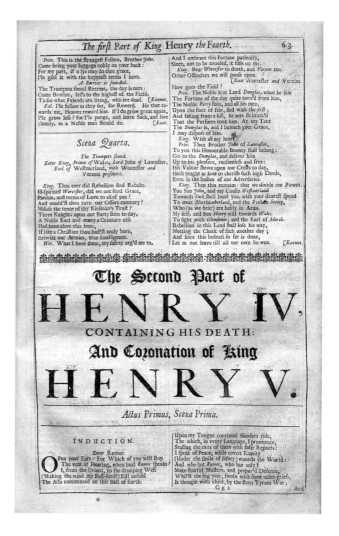

Over a number of years, Herringman began accumulating elements of the rights in Shakespeare's works. In 1685, working in conjunction with Richard Bentley—and with Edward Brewster and Richard Chiswell drawn in as, effectively, junior partners—Herringman published the Fourth Folio. Work on the volume was carried out at three different printshops, resulting in a somewhat inconsistent visual style across the book as a whole. A notable departure from the previous Folios was that, in the comedies and histories, the printers abandoned the principle that new plays should start on a new page, with the result that, in many places, one play begins immediately after the previous text ends. This often leads to a high degree of inelegance in the *mise-en-page*. A notable example is the transition from *1 Henry IV* to *2 Henry IV* (fig. 1.7). For the most part, the

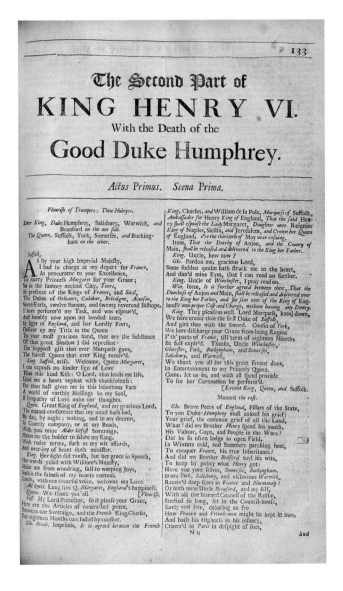

FIGURE 1.8 A sample opening of one of the pages included in the so-called "Fifth Folio," showing the distinctive lack of rules at the sides and bottom of the page. Folger Shakespeare Library, S2915 Fo.4 no.28, leaf 2N1 recto (p. 133).

tragedies (and apocrypha) avoid this practice (the one exception is *Othello*), but we also find some notable errors in this section of the text, such as the title "*the tragedy of Hamlet rpince of Denmark.*" The disruption to the act and scene structure of the plays that we have noted in the first three Folios is carried forward again into the text of the Fourth.

One notable feature of the Fourth Folio is that one of the firms of printers involved in producing it seems to have shortchanged Herringman and his colleagues by failing to print up the correct number of copies of the section that was assigned to them (Hansen and Rasmussen 2017; Lemley et al., chap. 6 in this volume). This discrepancy was discovered when the final copies of the edition were being assembled, with the result that another printer was brought in to produce the missing sheets. Copies of the Fourth Folio that include such made-up sheets are easy to spot, as the new printers departed from the model that had been in place since the First Folio, whereby the text columns were boxed in with rule at the top and bottom of the page and at either side of the columns. The newly printed pages omitted the bottom rule and the rules at the far left and far right of the page, giving the page a distinctive look (fig. 1.8). These sheets are thought to have been printed around 1700 and editions of the text that include the sheets are sometimes referred to as the "Fifth" Folio.

The Herringman-Bentley text was the last edition produced in the folio format and would be the last single volume edition of the collected plays to be issued for some considerable time. From the beginning of the eighteenth century onward, multivolume collected editions would be favored, partly for ease of use (the folio volume being rather large and weighty) and partly, in the longer run, to facilitate the growth of evermore extensive annotation and the accretion of supplementary materials. Thus, over time, the Shakespeare text—containable in a series of single volume editions for the duration of the seventeenth century—would grow and grow until, by 1803, the Samuel Johnson-George Steevens-Isaac Reed edition had reached twenty-one volumes.

We might close our consideration of the Folios here by casting our minds back to that day in 1593 when Shakespeare, the theaters closed, crossed the threshold of Richard Field's printshop, clutching the manuscript sheets of *Venus and Adonis* in his hand. Might he and Field have made small talk about Stratford acquaintances before Field cast his eyes over the text Shakespeare offered him? Might there have been a slight flicker of a raised eyebrow, a gentle furrowing of the brows on Field's part when he looked at the proffered text; he was, after all, not much known for publishing poetry and, in fact, mostly concentrated on work as a printer rather than as a publisher. In the end, of course, he did agree to issue the poem, having, presumably, settled on a price with Shakespeare. Could either of them have foreseen in that moment, as they struck their bargain, that from this first instance of Shakespeare publishing, such extraordinary industry would follow, from the four monumental Folios of the seventeenth century through to the latest digital editions of our own era?

CHAPTER 2

Paper, Type, and Labor
Making the First Folio

Claire M. L. Bourne

Mr. William Shakespeares Comedies, Histories, & Tragedies, the weighty printed collection of thirty-six plays and prefatory matter commonly referred to as the First Folio, was styled by its makers and subsequent commentators as a textual reliquary for Shakespeare's plays: his printed dramatic corpus as a proxy for his living likeness. As John Milton wrote in an encomium printed at the start of the second folio edition (published in 1632), the textual object containing Shakespeare's plays (even in its iterated form) was "a lasting Monument" indelibly inscribed with the playwright's "easie numbers" and "Delphicke lines" (sig. πA2r). Milton esteemed it an "unvalued Booke," by which he meant that the volume was invaluable, or priceless (*OED*, "unvalued," *adj*. 1a).

This chapter pulls us away from such metaphor and marketing to consider the bookishness of the codex by which Shakespeare's plays first became a single (if not singular) physical whole. It first considers the materials and labor used to print the book. Then, it moves to the typographic protocols that made Shakespeare's writing for a theatrical environment readable in print as plays. It ends by considering how the accidents of printing affected the book's production, and how they stand as a reminder of the fact that much of Shakespeare's greatness depends on the admirable and imperfect processes—both human and machine—of what Joseph Moxon, in 1683, called "Typographie," or the art of printing "*from the beginning to the end*" (sig. B3v).

MATERIALS AND LABOR

Each copy of the First Folio is a carefully designed object made of paper, ink, and type from human hands and toil. The single-volume edition was printed on a moveable-type handpress by a variety of printshop workers, including typesetters, press operators, proof-readers, and apprentices. The printing and assembly of the book was overseen by William Jaggard, along with his son Isaac, at their printing house in the Barbican, located in a parish just north of the London city walls. The impressively large folio was made by English people in the English metropole; however, the type and paper used to produce it were imported from the continent. Even though the Folio has been widely celebrated for consolidating, preserving, and even sanctifying Shakespeare as a canonical English author, it is not a straightforwardly English book (de Grazia and Stallybrass 1993, 280–82).

The word "folio" refers to the configuration of paper that makes up the book, otherwise known as the book's format: an assemblage of 224 sheets each folded once to create two leaves, or four pages (see Tara Lyons's chapter in this volume on "format"; the First Folio also contains six half sheets, for a total of 227 sheets [Willoughby 1932, 11]). To get even more technical, the book is a "folio in sixes," a structure that is formed by gathering three folded sheets, each of four pages, and nesting them one inside the next (fig. 2.1). These twelve-page gatherings were then stacked on top of each other to create a three-dimensional rectangular block of paper—and the first purpose-made printed folio collection of English commercial-theater plays.

The paper used for the project, which came from different stocks, was imported from the continent, most likely from northern France (Blayney 1991, 9; Bidwell 2002, 588; Hailey 2011, 13–14; Hansen 2014, 112–32). This was not unusual. Almost all books printed in England before the late seventeenth-century were made of continental paper stock, because cheaper production costs and more efficient distribution made it more affordable than English-made paper (Bidwell 2002, 584–88). It was only in the late 1600s that the English papermaking industry started to compete with imports, a shift born from the growing demand for printing paper along with new economic incentives and government protections (Bidwell 2002, 592–94; Blayney 1991, 9). While the Folio was a luxury item (costing about fifteen shillings unbound, compared to six pence for a single-title quarto playbook, at retail), the paper used for the project was of medium quality, perhaps to help keep production costs in check (Blayney 1991, 28, 9). Still, the Folio was a rather large book, not just in thickness but in terms of width and height. This is because it was printed on crown paper (named for the watermark used to distinguish it from other sizes), with each sheet measuring

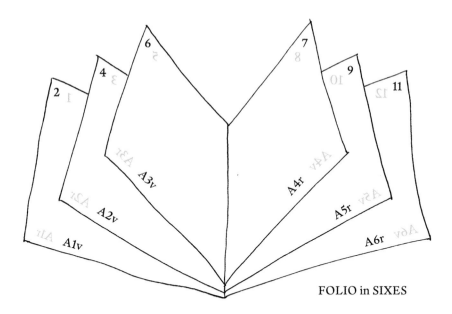

FIGURE 2.1   The First Folio was structured as a series of gatherings of three sheets (or six leaves, or twelve pages), with a few exceptions. It is therefore known as a "folio in sixes." Image by Claire M. L. Bourne.

about 18″ by 13¾″ (Hailey 2011, 8). Given that the sheet was folded once after printing and allowing for some trimming to smooth rough deckle edges, the largest copies of the Folio that survive measure about 13½″ by 8¾″ (Blayney 1991, 9). Copies of the Folio not in their original bindings are actually smaller than this since their leaves were trimmed again when rebound. In 1633, just a year after the second folio edition of Shakespeare's plays came to press, the antitheatricalist William Prynne complained that "Shackspeers Plaies are printed in the *best* Crowne paper, far better than most Bibles" (Prynne 1633, sig. **6v, emphasis added). Prynne's critical appraisal was part description and part rhetorical flourish—and could be referring to the First as well as the Second Folio. By the time the second edition went into production, the publishing syndicate may have been more confident that the book would sell and therefore more willing to invest in better quality paper of the same size. For the First Folio, however, the outlay for paper costs has been estimated to be one-third of the overall budget for the project, a bit less than the typical half, perhaps due to the additional cost of labor required for typesetting the plays in a tricky, type-dense two-column format (Bidwell 2002, 588). Steven Galbraith has calculated that it was cheaper (in terms of paper) to print Shakespeare's plays in folio format, rather than quarto (2010, 64–66).

The Folio's paper was handmade from linen rags recycled from household textiles. These were sourced from all around Europe and consolidated in the papermills of France, Italy, and elsewhere (Craig 2020, 32–34; de Grazia and Stallybrass 1993, 280–82). Rags cut from old clothing and sheets were used (again and again) to clean household surfaces and were thus repeatedly laundered. As Heidi Craig explains, once linen rags wore out as cleaning implements, they were "ideal for papermaking, since tattered, weak, and tender rags would ferment more easily, respond more readily to beating and grinding, and drain more quickly than the tough, strong fibres of raw flax or new linens" (2020, 32). Here, Craig is referring to steps in the papermaking process whereby well-used linen rags, collected by predominantly female ragpickers, were pounded to a pulp and then transferred to a vat of water. The resulting infusion was known as "stuff." The papermaker, assisted by other paper-mill personnel, would dunk a paper mould—a rectangular wooden frame made of wires arranged at right angles to each other—into the stuff-filled vat. Wide-spaced wires—called chain lines—ran parallel to the shorter side of the frame, and narrow-spaced wires—called laid lines—ran parallel to the longer side of the frame. Moulds frequently also featured watermarks—generated by bending wires into a recognizable shape, such as the crown found in the paper stocks used for the First and Second Folios. Wet stuff would be scooped up and agitated to even out the lumps and to let the water drain. The vatman would then pass the mould on to a laborer (called a coucher) who would press the drained pulp into a sheet of felt and then onto a stack of alternating paper and felt (called a post) to dry further. When the post reached 250 sheets, it would be pressed to squeeze out excess water. Sheets were then hung up to dry (see Craig 2020, 32; Hailey 2010, 9–10). There was also the process of sizing the paper once dry, which involved applying a thin coating (made, in part, from vegetable starches or, more commonly, animal gelatin) to the surface of the page to prevent printing ink from bleeding through the paper and ensure a crisp impression (Garlick 1986). Sheets of paper primed for printing ink (itself a product of "minerals, soot, and vegetable and animal colorings"; physical exertion; and, it was believed, a knowledge of the so-called dark arts [Johns 2010, 107]) were a necessary condition for the Folio's (or any printed book's) existence. They were one of the means by which Shakespeare's dramatic corpus could be made manifest as a readable object in the world.

The purchase of sheets for the project—227 sheets per copy multiplied by the estimated 750 copies that made up the edition equals 170,250 sheets of paper—would have required a considerable financial outlay for the book's publishers (see Andrew Murphy's chapter in this volume on the publication of the Folios). Indeed, the Folio was among the largest books to be produced by William

Jaggard's printing business and one of the largest folios on the market in 1623, period (Higgins 2022, 86). Besides the cost of paper and labor, not to mention the enormous investment of time, without any firm guarantee of profit, the other material challenge of producing a book this large was type supply. Every letter, number, punctuation mark, symbol, and blank space in the Folio represents a discrete piece of metal alloy type, each one of them set by hand. The Folio's two-column layout meant that each page contained a greater density of text (and thus required more physical type to be set at any one time) than if the playtexts had been presented in a single column—and even more could fit using Jaggard's "pica" roman compared to the slightly larger "English" roman type used in the one-column printing of Ben Jonson's plays in 1616 (Donovan 1991, 33). What this meant is that the job could only be executed by a printing outfit that had a substantial inventory of the right kind of type.

Jaggard had been active as a printer for a quarter century before he and his son Isaac supervised the printing of the First Folio. By the early 1620s, the Jaggards' stock of type was ample enough to support the printing of Shakespeare's plays. Careful logistics allowed printing to proceed with just two sheets of type (that is, two two-page formes of type) set at a time: after the proofing and printing of one sheet was finished, the next forme would move through the press while type from the first was redistributed and reused to set the next sheet in order (Jowett 2011, 17–19). In other words, Jaggard did not need to have enough type for a whole play, or even a whole twelve-page gathering (which would have required well over fifty-four thousand type sorts, exclusive of spaces). He only needed enough type for four pages—roughly eighteen thousand characters plus spacing material—to keep work flowing.*

The type used for the playtexts came from a pica roman fount. "Pica" now commonly refers to a standard unit of measurement used in printing (1/6 of an inch), but it also refers to a size of type during the handpress era. Although type size was never officially standardized during the seventeenth century, English printers amassed inventories of several different sizes of type, which they identified by names such as "small pica," "pica," "English," and so forth (Gaskell 1995, 13–14). The face of the pica type (that is, the raised image of the letter or number or other character) measured approximately 4 mm, while the body of the type (that is, the metal block onto which the face was cast) was slightly larger

---

*I have calculated that an average page (without act or scene divisions) uses about 4,400 to 4,600 pieces of type (exclusive of spacing material). Each forme that went through the press consisted of two type-set pages, which means that about nine-thousand pieces of type were needed per forme. If one forme was being set while the other was being proofed and printed, then somewhere in the ballpark of eighteen-thousand discrete pieces of type (not including spacing) were required.

at 4.2 mm. The italic type used for speech prefixes, stage directions, and proper nouns within dialogue is the same body size.

Like the paper stock used for the book, the type employed in printing the Folio came from Europe and is almost certainly Dutch in origin (Pollard 1909, 132). Most of it was imported decades before the Folio came to press. Some had been in Jaggard's inventory for at least fifteen years. It once belonged to the printer James Roberts, who had printed the first quarto of *The Merchant of Venice* and the second edition of *Titus Andronicus* in 1600, as well as the second quarto of *Hamlet* in 1604/5. Roberts had inherited the type from John Charlewood, who had printed the first editions of John Lyly's *Endymion* (1591) and *Gallathea* (1592). This type had therefore long been proximate to dramatic textual production. Roberts had connections to London's theater scene, having also once held the monopoly for printing playbills, which Jaggard would eventually secure for himself in 1615 after first trying (but failing) in 1602. After a couple of years of working in his own small Barbican printing house around the turn of the century, Jaggard bought Roberts's printing operation, including presses and type in 1606 and transferred his business into Roberts's larger former premises just down the street (Higgins 2022, 80–81). Jaggard had already used a combination of his own pica, as well as type he inherited from Roberts in the Shakespeare quartos that he printed in partnership with Thomas Pavier in 1619. As A. W. Pollard first pointed out, the pica used for the Folio is "sometimes found" in the 1619 quartos "mixed with upper-case letters [. . .], of a slightly larger face, from the old fount, of practically the same body, inherited by Jaggard from Roberts and by Roberts from Charlewood" (1909, 132). Some of the large italics used for running titles and in the Folio's preliminaries can be traced back to "the time of John Day," who was active as a printer in the mid-sixteenth century. It was at Roberts's old location on the corner of Aldersgate Street and the Barbican that the First Folio would be printed within two decades of Jaggard setting up shop there. Shakespeare's dramatic textual corpus would therefore come into being with a combination of type that had already been used to print countless other books and pieces of textual, even theatrical, ephemera (Hinman 1963, 1:16–25; Blayney 1991, 4–7; Smith 2015, 146).

Although William and Isaac Jaggard oversaw the printing of the Folio, the book's actual contents—that is, the combination of inky characters and blank spaces that make up "the text"—were generated physically by printshop workers called typesetters, or compositors (on the number and identities of the Folio's compositors, see: Walker 1953; Hinman 1963, 1:180–225; and Blayney 1991, 9–11; see Masten 2016 for a critique of "compositor studies"). Working from either handwritten manuscripts or marked-up printed editions as base texts for the

FIGURE 2.2 Every letter, number, punctuation mark, symbol, and blank space in the First Folio represents an individual piece of type, set by hand. All inked characters feature a raised face (here, "A") on top of a metal alloy body. Photo by Claire M. L. Bourne.

final printed products, these workers assembled individual type sorts—small, skinny pieces of metal alloy with a raised mirror-image glyph (letter, number, and so forth) on top—into words, lines, and ultimately blocks of text that could be inked and impressed on paper (see Maguire 1999, 438–44 for a lively account of this labor) (fig. 2.2). Every blank space—every indent, every space between words and lines—also had to be set individually by hand using slightly shorter pieces of type without a raised symbol on top (for indents and spaces between words) and horizontal spacers of varying heights called leading (to produce blank lines and space between lines). Pieces of type would have been organized in two cases, which were subdivided into compartments for each character. The top case (or upper case) contained the capital letters, while the bottom case (or lower case) contained the small letters (fig. 2.3). This process of textual production is a form of relief printing, a technique where the surface to be printed (here, letters, numbers, punctuation marks, ligatures, and other glyphs) is raised and thus isolated from the parts of the set type that would remain uninked and thus be rendered as "blank."

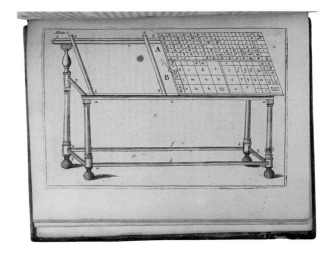

FIGURE 2.3 Type from a fount was organized and stored in an upper case (mostly capital letters) and a lower case (mostly small letters). After a forme had been printed and was no longer necessary, the type would be cleaned and redistributed into the cases for reuse. Joseph Moxon, *Mechanick Exercises: Or, the Doctrine of Handy-works. Applied to the Art of Printing* (1683), sig. D2v. Harry Ransom Center, University of Texas at Austin, Z 244 A2 M905 v. 2 copy 2.

Type set by hand bit-by-bit in a composing stick (a small, adjustable, metal handheld container) would be transferred onto a galley (a large wooden board) (fig. 2.4). Then, when the type block was complete, it would be tied together with string and transferred onto a correcting stone, where it (along with the other pages to be printed on the same side of the sheet) would be locked into a frame known as a "chase." Within the chase, the blocks of type would be surrounded by rectangular pieces of wood called "furniture" and long wedges around the edges. Finally, "quoins"—that is, small wedges—would be "driven home with a mallet and 'shooting stick'" between the larger wedges and the inside edge of the chase to create tension and hold the type in place (Gaskell 1972, 80). The combination of chase, type, furniture, and quoins is known as a "forme" (fig. 2.5). With everything locked in place, the forme was, in the words of Philip Gaskell, "virtually a solid slab of wood and metal . . . and could be moved about or lifted without the type falling out" (1972, 80). The forme could then be transferred to the bed of the press, where a sticky printing ink was applied to the surface of the type using large hemispheric leather-covered ink balls (sometimes soaked in urine to keep the leather pliable). A slightly damp sheet of paper would be placed on the press's tympan, a frame covered tightly with fabric set at an angle to the printing bed. A frisket (a piece of paper with an area cut out that matched the size of the area to be printed) closed by hinge over the tympan and then, together, they were folded parallel with bed and rolled over the forme. Workmen then pulled a lever to lower the platen (the flat printing plate) to create pressure between type and paper and thus an inked impression. Pulling too hard would create type "bite" through the sheet. The goal was to apply just enough pressure for the type to "kiss" the paper. Because the paper needed to be slightly damp to make it more receptive to the type, the sheets would then be hung to dry on wooden racks.

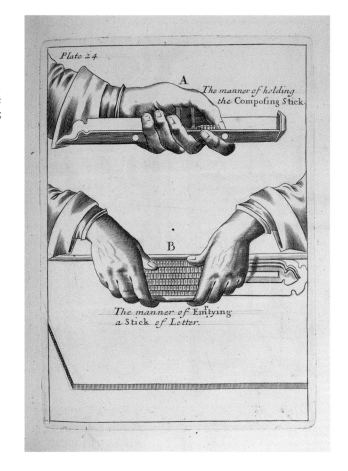

FIGURE 2.4 Compositors used a portable metal composing stick to set type several lines at a time before transferring it to the galley. They needed to set the text in reverse (right to left) so that it printed in the correct reading order (left to right). Harry Ransom Center, University of Texas at Austin, Z 244 A2 M905 v. 2 copy 2.

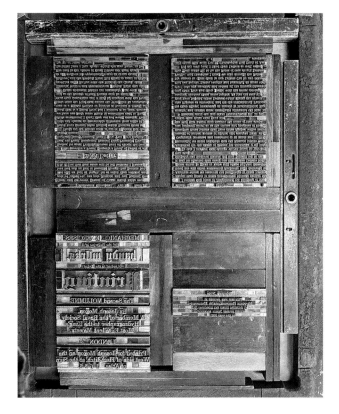

FIGURE 2.5 A quarto forme locked up for printing. Type is surrounded by furniture (the wooden blocks) and keyed quoins (the devices with circular keyholes) inside a chase. The type of quoin pictured here, in which a key turned in the keyhole would expand the device to create tension, postdates the First Folio, for which quoins consisted of small wedges forced between the chase and larger, longer wedges to lock up the forme. A folio forme would feature two (rather than four) blocks of type to make up its two pages. These would be oriented from one long side of the chase (top of the type page) to the other (bottom of the type page). Photo by permission of Joshua Eckhardt.

This muscular process had to be repeated for each side of every sheet. This means that the lever had to be pulled more than 330,000 times to produce all 750 copies of the Folio—a book made from just over 220 sheets (440 sides). Although the First Folio was marketed in such a way that highlighted Shakespeare's wit and intellectual prowess, its existence is due as much to printing-house brawn as it is to the playwright's brains.

DESIGN

For all the critical discussion about how the contingencies of printing interfered with the book's promise to present "true Originall" versions of Shakespeare's theatrical visions, the First Folio is a thoughtfully designed book. Its overall design shows that its makers considered both the aesthetics and practicalities of a project so large and innovative as a single volume of thirty-six plays, a genre that required special typographic affordances to help readers encounter the texts as mediations of theatrical content (i.e., *as plays*) rather than as poetry or some other form of imaginative writing. It is worth acknowledging that book design and page design in the handpress era were always, to some degree, aspirational given the constraints of available materials and the fallibility of human labor and mechanical processes. Printing plays—indeed, a whole corpus of plays—written for performance in a multisensory playhouse environment so that their uniquely theatrical attributes could be legible to readers presented an additional challenge.

The first opening (or two-page spread) of the First Folio immediately calls attention to its bookishness (fig. 2.6). On the left-hand verso (back of the page), a commendatory poem by contemporary playwright Ben Jonson, printed in a large roman font, directs readers' eyes to the recto (front) of the facing page, from which an imposing, carefully engraved portrait of Shakespeare, situated between the book's title at the top of the page and the names of its makers at the bottom, peers up (see Erin Blake's chapter in this volume on the portrait). Jonson's encomium invites readers to look at "this figure" (the engraving), purposely "put" "here" to present an image of Shakespeare as he lived. Jonson laments that the engraver could not "dravv[...]" Shakespeare's "vvit / As well in brasse, as he hath hit / His face." If only the engraver could have captured Shakespeare's mind using the materials of his art ("brasse" refers to the metal plate used to generate the portrait), the engraving would be the best, most authentic one ever made. The poem ends with Jonson revising his initial entreaty for readers to look at the "Picture." He suggests that the only way to really see Shakespeare is to bypass the picture and "looke / . . . on . . . his Booke." Put simply, Jonson's "To the Reader"

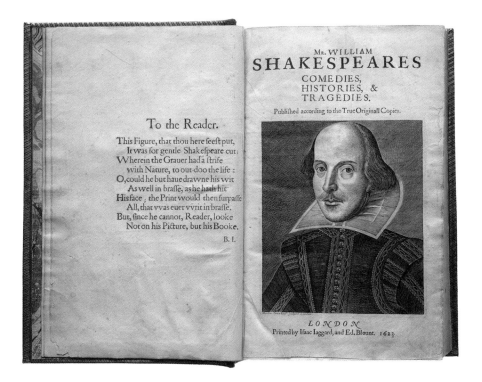

FIGURE 2.6   The first opening (two-page spread) of the First Folio includes a poem from Ben Jonson, inviting readers to look at the portrait on the facing title page, but also to turn the page and read the book. Folger Shakespeare Library, STC 22273 Fo.1 no.05, sigs. ⁿA1v–ⁿA1+1.

is an invitation to turn the page: physically interacting with the book is the only way to know and understand Shakespeare.

The book's title page typographically privileges Shakespeare's surname as well as the three genres in which he excelled as a playwright. "SHAKESPEARES" (a possessive which asserts a posthumous claim to the texts that follow) is printed using the largest type in the book—it appears elsewhere only in play titles and the title of the "catalogue" (or table of contents) in the book's preliminaries. Stacked underneath the playwright's name is the list of genres that provide an organizing principle for the book's contents: "COMEDIES, / HISTORIES, & / TRAGEDIES." Each generic label is afforded its own line, thereby asserting a kind of equivalence among them. The use of an ampersand (&) instead of the word "and" may also be purposeful—to eliminate distraction from the symmetry and balance of the generic triad. Below the title appears a key claim supporting the book's value: the comedies, histories, and tragedies mentioned in the title are "published according to the True Originall Copies." Even though conventions of capitalization had not yet settled by the 1620s, the capitalization of the

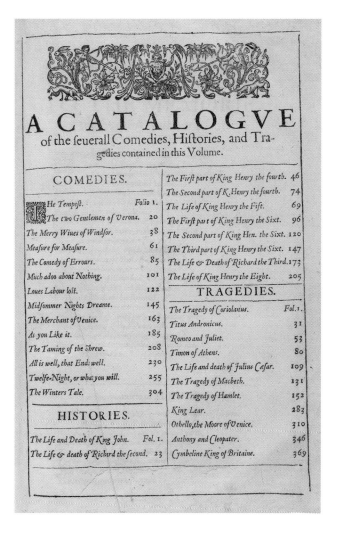

FIGURE 2.7 The page of the First Folio's prefatory matter that gives an overview of the book's contents and (with its double-column format and textual divisions) anticipates the layout of the playtexts themselves. Used with kind permission of the Free Library of Philadelphia, Rare Book Department, RBD EL SH15M 1623, sig. ⁋6r.

noun and its modifiers intensifies the idea that book contains versions of the plays that are "shakespeares"—the manuscripts used as the basis for the plays found inside are, quite literally, author-ized.

What follows the title page is a series of preliminary texts: a dedicatory epistle printed in large italics; an address to *"the great Variety of Readers,"* presented in a roman font slightly smaller than the preceding epistle; and a collection of commendatory poems set using a combination of roman and italic fonts, all variously larger than the pica roman and italic type used for the playtexts. In addition to a page listing "The Names of the Principall Actors / in all these Playes" in two columns, the book also opens with "a catalogve / of the seuerall Comedies, Histories, and Tragedies contained in this Volume." The *mise-en-page* of the catalogue page anticipates the aesthetic features of the playtexts to follow: printed content enclosed inside a rectangle generated by inked impressions of

FIGURE 2.8   The first page of *Henry the Sixth, Part 1*, showing the running header, title box (including ornament plus title), and inaugural act and scene heading typical of all opening pages of playtexts in the book. Used with kind permission of the Free Library of Philadelphia, Rare Book Department, RBD EL SH15M 1623, sig. k2v.

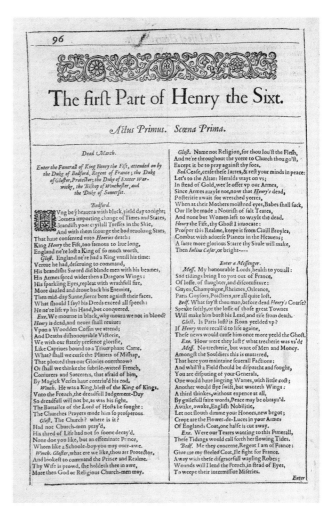

thin brass rules and divided into two columns, with a title box ranging the width of the rectangle created by the rules at the top of the page (fig. 2.7). The content (here, names of plays and the pages on which they appear) is further separated into sections with uppercase roman headings announcing the genre of the plays listed below it, set off by one column-width brass rule above and one below. This same technique of fashioning headings is used in the playtexts for most act and scene divisions.

Moving beyond the varied design of the Folio's prefatory matter, readers could settle into a more predictable set of typographic protocols. What follows here, then, is a description of the design conventions used to render the playtexts in print. As is the case with the "catalogue" page, every type-page is bounded on the top, bottom, left, and right by thin inked lines that together form a box (figs. 2.8, 2.9, 2.10). These lines were created by pliable, inked brass rules. They

FIGURE 2.9 The playtext (here, a page from *A Midsummer Night's Dream*) is set using pica roman type and presented in two columns of sixty-six lines (plus catchword). Stage directions, speech prefixes, and proper names appear in italics. A running header announces the name of the play and page number. Here, the page number is incorrect—it should read "153" but has not been changed in the skeleton forme. Used with kind permission of the Free Library of Philadelphia, Rare Book Department, RBD EL SH15M 1623, sig. N5r.

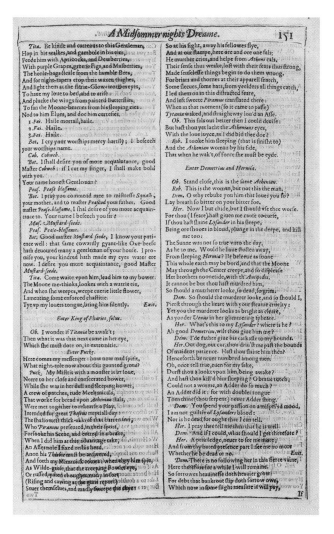

delimit the area of the page where typographic content would appear (approximately 282 mm × 171 mm) and, in so doing, also delineate distinct margins (the blank space outside the ruled box), which many readers of the book would take as an invitation to inscribe their names and other notes (some related to the content and some not) (fig. 2.11).

The typographic protocols for announcing the start of a new play are manifold. On the first page of every play, two parallel lines cut horizontally across the portrait-oriented box roughly a quarter to a third of the way down the page, effectively creating a smaller landscape-oriented box in the top quarter or third of the page to accommodate the play's title, which is set (sometimes in large uppercase roman, sometimes in a combination of large uppercase and lowercase roman), in all instances, beneath one of five horizontal headpiece ornaments. Above the ornament is another horizontal rule running parallel to the line at

FIGURE 2.10 The design of the final pages of playtexts were handled differently, depending on how much text remained to be set. In cases where a little bit of remaining text left lots of space (*upper left*), an ornamented tailpiece was used for both practical and aesthetic reasons. In cases where the remainder text filled more than half of the page (*upper right*), what follows is a version of "FINIS." with rules above and below. The final page of *Much Ado About Nothing* (*lower right*) appears on the first page of gathering L and is severely cramped due to a miscalculation with casting off. Used with kind permission of the Free Library of Philadelphia, Rare Book Department, BD EL SH15M 1623, sigs. I2v, E6v, and L1r.

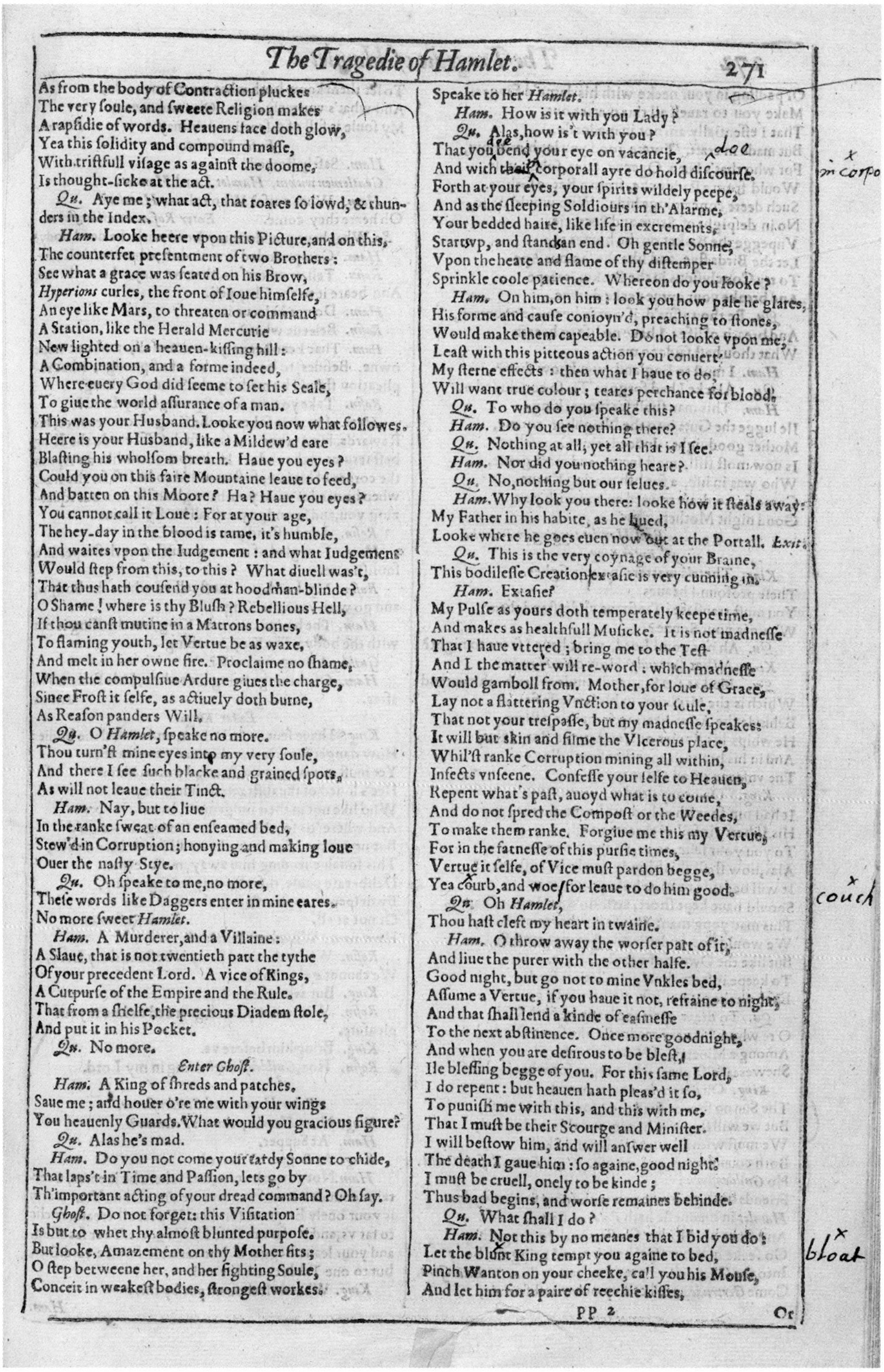

FIGURE 2.11 John Milton used the margins of his copy of the First Folio to note variant readings. Here, he suggests alternatives to three words that appear in the "closet scene" in *Hamlet*. Used with kind permission of the Free Library of Philadelphia, Rare Book Department, RBD EL SH15M 1623, sig. pp2r. See also figures 5.3 and 5.5.

the top of the type-page box that creates a strip of space for a running header. On the first page of each play (with a couple of exceptions), this space contains a page number in the outer corner. In between the parallel rules underneath the title appears some version of the "Act 1, Scene 1" formula printed in medium-sized italic font: "*Actus primus, Scena prima.*"; "*Actus primus.*"; "*Actus primus. Scæna Prima.*"; "*Actus Primus, Scæna Prima.*"; "*Actus Primus. Scæna Prima.*"; and so forth. Every play opens with a variation of this formula, whether or not it is subsequently divided into acts and scenes. The remaining two-thirds or three-quarters of the type-page is divided into two columns by a line (generated by a series of shorter brass rules) running vertically down the middle. These smaller rectangles serve as containers (or frames) for the playtext itself. In most cases, each play opens with a centered stage direction set in italics and a speech tag also set in italics; with few exceptions, the speech tag is either centered over the first speech, or indented on the line above the first speech. The first speech of every play also begins with an ornamented initial.

A *typical* page of playtext, then, is hemmed on all four sides by rules. At the top of the page, a running header created by the horizontal rule running close and parallel to the top of the box displays the title of the play (centered and set using the same italic font as the opening act and scene heading) and a page number in roman type situated inside the header box nearest the outside edge of the page. For plays with longer titles (usually those that designate their genre in the title), the first half of the title—such as, "*The Tragedie of*"—appears in the running header on the verso (left page) and the second half of the title—such as, "*Antony and Cleopatra*"—appears on the recto (right page) of the page opening. The rest of the text box underneath the running header is divided into columns, again by a vertical line made from a sequence of smaller brass rules. Each column of text totals about sixty-six lines of type with a catchword (which indicates the first word of the next page) at the bottom of the right-hand column. A signature mark also appears on the recto (front) of the first three leaves in each gathering. Because the pages of the book were not printed consecutively (1, 2, 3, 4, etc.), the numbers in these signature marks helped ensure that the finished sheets would be folded and gathered in such a way that the printed pages ended up in the right order. The letters in signature marks (A, B, C, D, etc.) helped make sure that the gatherings themselves were assembled in the correct sequence.

The final page of each play differs from one play to the next depending on how much of the two columns the remaining playtext fills. In all cases, that remainder is distributed evenly across the two columns, so that both columns finish flush with each other. Underneath, a horizontal rule underlines the ending of the play. The word "FINIS." (centered and set in uppercase roman) formalizes the end. Another horizontal rule is placed below this all-caps announcement to box it in. Below this, in some instances, appears one of three large inverted triangular tailpiece ornaments. Setting ornaments in this space was, first and foremost, a practical consideration rather than strictly an aesthetic choice: leaving a swath of a page blank (that is, set with spacing material that had a lower profile than raised type) would leave the sheet of paper unsupported under the load of the press. Printers would sometimes use "bearing type" for this purpose: that is, uninked type "intended to support paper which, due to accidental inking or too vigorous pulling of the press, leaves an inked or blind (uninked but embossed) impression" (Smyth 2017, 87). In many cases, the Jaggards and their compositors opted to use inked ornamental tailpieces to provide this support. In a few cases, a dramatis personae was added at the end of the text when there was additional space to fill, such as at the end of *Othello*, where we get a list of "the Actors" (actually, characters) as well as a tailpiece. The appearance of these ornaments in otherwise "blank" space also has the aesthetic effect of tapering, reinforcing the effect of finality.

All these structural elements of the book's page design—rules, columns, headpieces, titles, tailpieces, ornamented initials, running headers—determine the limits of the playtext itself: where it begins, ends, is divided, and appears in the first place. It is easy to take for granted the way the playtext looks on the page—it obviously looks like a playtext to modern eyes. But that "look" is the result of sustained experiments by printers, publishers, playwrights, and other printshop personnel with adapting textual matter that was initially designed to be embodied and performed, into textual matter fit for reading (see Bourne 2020). The typographic protocols for playtexts published in the First Folio reflect how conventions for mediating (however imperfectly) the non-lexical energies of plays in print were settling by the 1620s.

In the first place, different fonts are used to distinguish dialogue (here, pica roman) from speech prefixes and stage directions (both printed in italic) (figs. 2.8, 2.9, 2.10). Such typographic differentiation makes the distinction between what is being said and who is saying it (along with information about the nonverbal business that may accompany it) immediately visible. Speech prefixes, which announce who is speaking, are more often than not abbreviated to their first few letters. This strategy of type economization was not at all unusual for printed plays at the time, but it would have required readers to defer to entrance stage directions for the full names of characters (or to dramatis personae, when available). As for stage directions, those describing entrances and other significant stage business are typically centered (but sometimes ranged to the right of dialogue), while exit/exeunt directions are usually right-justified. Italics are used to effect typographic differentiation in other clever (yet conventional) circumstances. Besides being used for proper names in dialogue, the most notable use of italics is to visually isolate songs, letters, proclamations, and other discrete textual genres from spoken dialogue. The italics signal that these units of text are of a different kind than real-time speech. Within the fiction, they are rehearsed, read, and voiced (as in, they relay a voice other than the person doing the singing, reading, or proclaiming). It has also been suggested that the use of italic type for these inset texts mediates their simultaneous connection to and separation from the play proper, in that they probably circulated separately from the handwritten playbook (which contained the script of the play) and other documents of performance at the same time as they were performed as part of the play (Stern 2009, 174–200).

Another convention of dramatic typography evident in the layout of dialogue is the placement of a blank space (or indent) before the speech prefix at the start of every new unit of dialogue. These indents signal changes in speakers, but they are also technically redundant given that speech prefixes serve the same function. So, why are they there? The use of the indent to indicate when speech shifts from one character to another is a holdover from the early sixteenth-century practice of placing a pilcrow (¶) at the start of a new speech to mark a change of speaker in printed interludes (Bourne 2020, 70–72). Printed pilcrows themselves were, in general, a holdover from the scribal convention of situating an embellished *C* (or capitulum) at the start of a new unit of text. (Scribes would leave a double backslash—//—where a specialist called a rubricator would inscribe the *C*, usually in red, but sometimes in blue, ink. The combination of these symbols is what forms the more familiar ¶.) Early play printers then used it to help readers visualize the dialogic form of dramatic texts. Once its utility in this respect was no longer needed, and once longer plays strained printers' inventories of this glyph, it fell out of use and was replaced by an em-quad, or blank, which is recognizable to us today as an indent. The consistent use of indents in the First Folio thus effectively mediated the theatrical effect of changing voices using the materials of print.

Another noticeable design protocol in nineteen of the Folio's thirty-six playtexts is the combining of two horizontal, parallel, column-width rules to sandwich italicized act and scene headings (fig. 2.13). As noted above, all plays open with some version of an "*Actus primus. Scena Prima.*" heading that runs the width of the type-page. Together, these typographic complexes of italicized rubrics and horizontal lines divide the plays into smaller formal units (Hirsh 2002; Bourne 2020, 168–75). The specific placement of these divisions, even within playtexts that appear to have a complete set of divisions (which some do not), does not always align with our modern notion that textual divisions are proxies for a cleared stage. There is not space in this chapter to adjudicate the many apparent idiosyncrasies of division in the Folio. Suffice it to say that there is some consistency in the typographic presentation of these divisions, making it easier for readers to identify discrete units of the plays as they worked their way through, or around, the book.

The design protocols of the First Folio playtexts are clear and consistent and, for that reason, almost unremarkable. In the end, though, they support readers' encounters with the texts *as plays* in ways specific to printed drama. Deviation from these designs is almost always due to a physical contingency of printing, to which this chapter now turns.

ACCIDENTS

It is commonplace for book historians, especially those who study reading and reception, to note that no two copies of the First Folio are the same. They all bear unique traces of the people, places, and hazards they have met with along their circuitous, four-century-long journeys from the Jaggard printing house in London's Barbican neighborhood to their current whereabouts across the world (see Zachary Lesser's chapter in this volume on provenance and the challenge of counting extant copies of Shakespeare). But given the realities of moveable-type printing (which often required improvisation, correction, and adjustments due to human error and wear and tear on equipment), no two copies of the book have ever been the same, even before the assembled sheets were taken for trade or customized bindings and then exposed to their earliest readers. This final section illuminates some of the ways that the printing process led to variability among copies—and how this variability has been used to better understand the inner workings of the Jaggard printing operation (including the other books the Jaggards were printing while sheets for the First Folio were moving through the press).

As discussed above, the Folio was printed in units of three sheets called gatherings, or quires. Onto each sheet was printed four pages—two on one side and two on the other. The sheets were then folded and assembled one inside the next for a total of six leaves and twelve pages. The structure of the gathering required that pages 1 and 12 of the gathering had to be printed on one side of the outer-most sheet, while pages 2 and 11 had to be printed on the other side of that same sheet; pages 3 and 10 on one side, and pages 4 and 9 on the other side of the middle sheet; and pages 5 and 8 on one side, and pages 6 and 7 on the other side of the inner-most sheet (fig. 2.1). The type was set one side of a sheet (not one page) at a time, which meant, for instance, that pages 2 and 11 would be set at the same time and sent to press, while pages 1 and 12 were being set so that those pages were ready to print by the time pages 2 and 11 had finished their run. As mentioned above, the pair of type-set pages locked up in the chase and ready for printing on one side of a sheet is known as a forme.

All the playtext pages of the Folio (save first and last pages of plays) have the same typographic apparatus structuring the page: frame, running header, and medial line to delimit columns. Instead of re-setting these elements, this "skeleton forme" was reused (when work on the Folio proceeded uninterrupted) for each subsequent pair of pages—only page numbers and, if necessary, running titles had to be changed. In a few cases, compositors forgot to make these changes to the running header leading to errors in running titles and in pagination, some (but not all) of which would be corrected when the page was proofed (fig. 2.12). It appears that the skeleton forme used for first pages was also left standing as long as work on the Folio proceeded uninterrupted by other printing projects; the title and page number were changed, but the framing rules, the ornament in the title box, and the type for the "Act 1, Scene 1" formula with the horizontal rule beneath it remained.

Sheets were proofed at some stage in their print run. The press was stopped more than one hundred times to make corrections (Blayney 1991, 14). Stop-press corrections to running headers—and, more importantly, to the playtext itself—resulted in different versions of the same forme being printed: some were printed with the error and others were printed with the corrected text. But all those versions of the sheet made it into one copy of the book or another. Given the paper-intensive and expensive nature of the project, discarding part of a print run for relatively minor errors would have been far too costly. Indeed, early modern readers were much more error tolerant than our habituation to the hardened conventions of spelling and punctuation have made us (Smyth 2017, 77). This goes for proofing and stop-press corrections to the text of the plays themselves. Some copies of the Folio even preserve proof sheets—that is, the sheets run through the press and then manually marked up by the proofreader to note corrections that needed to be made before printing could continue (Blayney 1991, 16). Because sheets were shuffled when they were taken down from the drying racks and stacked for storage, and ultimately for assembly, sale, and binding, every extant copy of the Folio contains different combinations of corrected and uncorrected sheets. As Peter W. M. Blayney puts it: "No copy has all those pages in the final [corrected] state; none has so many in the earliest [uncorrected] state

The 2 Gentlemen of Verona

38   *The Merry Wives of Windsor.*

Be thou asham'd that I haue tooke vpon me,
Such an immodest rayment; if shame liue
In a disguise of loue?
It is the lesser blot modesty findes,
Women to change their shapes, then men their minds.
  Pro. Then men their minds? tis true: oh heuen, were man
But Constant, he were perfect; that one error
Fils him with faults: makes him run through all th'sins;
Inconstancy falls-off, ere it begins:
What is in *Siluia's* face, but I may spie
More fresh in *Iulia's*, with a constant eye?
  Val. Come, come: a hand from either:
Let me be blest to make this happy close:
'Twere pitty two such friends should be long foes.
  Pro. Beare witnes (heauen) I haue my wish for euer.
  Iul. And I mine.
  Out-l. A prize: a prize: a prize.
  Val. Forbeare, forbeare I say: It is my Lord the *Duke*.
Your Grace is welcome to a man disgrac'd,
Banished *Valentine*.
  Duke. Sir *Valentine*?
  Thu. Yonder is *Siluia*: and *Siluia's* mine.
  Val. Thurio giue backe; or else embrace thy death:
Come not within the measure of my wrath:
Doe not name *Siluia* thine: if once againe,
Verona shall not hold thee: heere she stands,
Take but possession of her, with a Touch:
I dare thee, but to breath vpon my Loue.
  Thur. Sir *Valentine*, I care not for her, I:
I hold him but a foole that will endanger
His Body, for a Girle that loues him not:
I claime her not, and therefore she is thine.
  Duke. The more degenerate and base art thou
To make such meanes for her, as thou hast done,
And leaue her on such slight conditions.

Now, by the honor of my Ancestry,
I doe applaud thy spirit, *Valentine*,
And thinke thee worthy of an Empresse loue:
Know then, I heere forget all former greefes,
Cancell all grudge, repeale thee home againe,
Plead a new state in thy vn-riual'd merit,
To which I thus subscribe: Sir *Valentine*,
Thou art a Gentleman, and well deriu'd,
Take thou by *Siluia*, for thou hast deseru'd her.
  Val. I thank your Grace, ye gift hath made me happy:
I now beseech you (for your daughters sake)
To grant one Boone that I shall aske of you.
  Duke. I grant it (for thine owne) what ere it be.
  Val. These banish'd men, that I haue kept withall,
Are men endu'd with worthy qualities:
Forgiue them what they haue committed here,
And let them be recall'd from their Exile:
They are reformed, ciuill, full of good,
And fit for great employment (worthy Lord.)
  Duke. Thou hast preuaild, I pardon them and thee:
Dispose of them, as thou knowst their deserts.
Come, let vs goe, we will include all iarres,
With Triumphes, Mirth, and rare solemnity.
  Val. And as we walke along, I dare be bold
With our discourse, to make your Grace to smile.
What thinke you of this Page (my Lord?)
  Duke. I think the Boy hath grace in him, he blushes.
  Val. I warrant you (my Lord) more grace, then Boy.
  Duke. What meane you by that saying?
  Val. Please you, Ile tell you, as we passe along,
That you will wonder what hath fortuned:
Come *Protheus*, 'tis your pennance, but to heare
The story of your Loues discouered.
That done, our day of marriage shall be yours,
One Feast, one house, one mutuall happinesse.   *Exeunt.*

The names of all the Actors.

Duke: *Father to Siluia.*
Valentine. } *the two Gentlemen.*
Protheus.
Anthonio: *father to Protheus.*
Thurio: *a foolish riuall to Valentine.*

Eglamoure: *Agent for Siluia in her escape.*
Host: *where Iulia lodges.*
Out-lawes *with Valentine.*
Speed: *a clownish seruant to Valentine.*
Launce: *the like to Protheus.*
Panthion: *seruant to Antonio.*
Iulia: *beloued of Protheus.*
Siluia: *beloued of Valentine.*
Lucetta: *waighting-woman to Iulia.*

FINIS.

THE

FIGURE 2.12   Compositors forgot to change the running title for *The Merry Wives of Windsor* in the skeleton forme when setting the last two pages of *The Two Gentlemen of Verona*. A reader has corrected the error. Used with kind permission of the Free Library of Philadelphia, Rare Book Department, RBD EL SH15M 1623, sig. D1v.

that it can be called an early copy. Furthermore, no two copies have yet been found to contain exactly the same mixture of early and late pages" (1991, 15). No materials—nor any labor—went to waste.

Other type-setting curiosities in the Folio can be explained by the Jaggards' pragmatic approach to printing a large book—one that required so many pieces of type per page—with a finite supply of type. Because nonconsecutive pages in a gathering had to be type-set and printed at the same time (that is, on the same side of the same sheet), Jaggard's compositors could not start at the beginning of the chunk of text and work through the twelve pages of a gathering *seriatim* (that is, in order). Doing so would have required more than three times the amount of type (as described above): type set for the first five pages would have been left standing until the compositors got through pages 6 and 7 and could redistribute that type to finally set page 8 in the same forme as page 5; page 9 in the same forme as page 4; and so on. Instead, they used a process called "casting off" to estimate how much text would fit on the first five pages of the gathering so that they could set the type "by formes." Based on those calculations, typesetting then started with pages 6 and 7, which were positioned consecutively on facing pages in the middle of the gathering (fig. 2.1). Once that forme was transferred to the press, compositing could begin for the opening containing pages 5 and 8 (to be printed on the reverse of the sheet containing pages 6 and 7). That forme would then move to the press, as the type used for pages 6 and 7 (all but the skeleton) was redistributed into the typecases so that pages 4 and 9 could be set.

This process was expeditious, but it also had risks. While the last seven pages of the gathering were set in order, the first five were set in reverse. Even slight miscalculations in the casting-off of the first five pages could result in two different issues for the compositors by the time they got to the first page of the gathering: being left with too much text and not enough space for it to fit; or being left with too much space and not enough text to fill it. For this reason, typographic anomalies born from space-saving or space-wasting techniques tend to be most pronounced on the first page or two of gatherings in the book: verse set as prose or prose set as verse (fig. 2.10c); single verse lines turned into two half lines to fill space; *Exit* directions (usually set on their own lines, just below the last line of the preceding speech) moved up to the right of that final line of dialogue or moved down another line by a blank line used for padding; the expansion or contraction of blank space around act and scene divisions; and, in the most extenuating circumstances, the addition or elimination of a whole stage direction (Smith 2015, 145). Even with this efficacious system of typesetting and redistribution (which gets type back into commission quickly), there remain instances in the Folio where the project's strain on type supply is evident. Laurie

Maguire has noted that printing plays, especially given "the frequency of character names," could overtax a printer's type inventory (1999, 445). The strain on uppercase italic *E* is especially pronounced, for example, in *King Lear*, where that letter is needed for "*Enter*" and "*Exit*," as well as for "*Edmund*" and "*Edgar*" (both in speech prefixes and stage directions) (fig. 2.13).

Another casualty of printing was damaged type (see the chapter by Samuel V. Lemley et al. in this volume on damaged type as bibliographical evidence). While badly damaged types were "*ordinarily* soon discarded," types that were "less seriously damaged" could "continue [...] in use indefinitely" (Hinman 1963, 1:61–2). During his detailed study of press variants in fifty-five copies of the First Folio at the Folger Shakespeare Library, Charlton Hinman identified six hundred distinctive type sorts with different degrees and kinds of damage (1963, 1:421–65). These types sustained damage through the routine mechanical processes of printing:

> One of many theoretically identical types becomes an individual through physical injury. Part of its face is broken away, or bent from its original shape, or slashed, or gouged, or nicked, or splayed, or otherwise so marred that subsequent impressions from it are sufficiently distinctive to be recognized. The damage appears usually to have been sustained during actual printing operations, while the type or type affected were locked up in a forme that was being machined. The immediate agent was in most instances a small body of foreign matter that somehow found its way on to the surface of the forme and was driven into the letterpress when the bar of the press was pulled and the platen forced down upon the type page under it. (1963, 1:54)

Hinman was able to track some of these damaged types, not only through the Folio but also to the 1619 Shakespeare quartos and other books that the Jaggards were printing between early 1622 and November 1623, at which point printing work on the Folio is believed to have been completed. The appearance of the same damaged type in other Jaggard books from the same eighteen-month period corroborates evidence of interrupted printing suggested by the suspension of repetition in skeleton formes (Greg 1955, 438–39; Blayney 1991, 5–7). As Hinman's colleague W. W. Greg explained: "When printing proceeds smoothly we find the skeleton formes repeating themselves in orderly fashion from quire to quire, and when this orderly repetition is broken, and fresh rules are introduced and running titles are reset, we may infer that there was some disturbance or interruption in the work" (435).

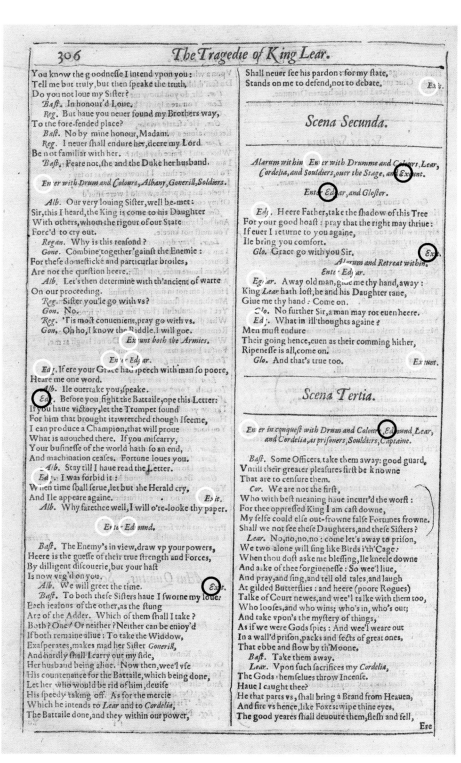

FIGURE 2.13 The frequency of "*Enter*," "*Exit*," and two character names beginning with *E* (Edgar and Edmund) at certain points in *King Lear* put strain on the supply of capital italic *E*. The problem is solved by supplementing the square italic *E* with an epsilon-style italic *E*, from another typeface. Used with kind permission of the Free Library of Philadelphia, Rare Book Department, RBD EL SH15M 1623, sig. ff1v.

Hinman made a key observation about the repetition of specific pieces of damaged type in the Folio itself—that is, an observation on which rests much of our understanding of how the Folio was printed. He noted that an individual type with distinctive damage never appeared twice on the same page or same forme but that it did sometimes appear in the same gathering, or quire (1963, 1:57). This, along with the layout curiosities around space-wasting and space-saving discussed above, led him to conclude that the gatherings were not set in order but rather through the economizing but risky process of casting off and setting by formes.

In terms of page design protocols, the other three seventeenth-century Shakespeare folios replicated the Jaggard two-column design, as did the 1647 folio collection of plays printed under the names of John Fletcher and Francis Beaumont. As typographers and historians of typography often note, readers are inherently resistant to design change, which may explain why the First Folio's typographic arrangements set the standard for drama folios until the early eighteenth century. The book—expensive both to produce and to buy—was a success, seeing a second edition come to press within a decade. While individual plays continued to be published—successfully—in quarto format, the typographic hallmark of the dramatic corpus was the large double-column page.

Milton was right that the First Folio is an "unvalued" book—but for reasons beyond its role in establishing Shakespeare's monumentality in literary history. It is hard to put a price on a book that stands as a touchstone in the history of dramatic typography. But it is equally difficult to put a price on the intellectual, imaginative, and physical labor expended in its making.

CHAPTER 3

The Droeshout Portrait and the Title Page

Erin C. Blake

The title page of the 1623 First Folio is iconic, so it is easy to overlook just how strange it must have appeared to its seventeenth-century readers. This is not a conventional early modern title page. For one thing, a portrait stares out from the center. For another, the title page represents a combination of two incompatible printing techniques: relief for the words and intaglio for the portrait. This chapter explores both oddities, and suggests that the publishers of the First Folio were attempting to produce an impressive title page on the cheap.

Before the advent of printed book covers in the nineteenth century, title pages did the work of enticing potential buyers. Instead of judging a book by its cover, early modern readers judged a book by its title page. For this reason, standard title pages needed to communicate more about what was inside the book than today's do. Most title pages provided information about the contents in words. For example, a book published the same year as Shakespeare's First Folio had the title: *The History of Xenophon, Containing the Ascent of Cyrus into the Higher Countries. Wherein is Described the Admirable Journey of Ten Thousand Grecians from Asia the Less into the Territories of Babylon, and their Retreat from Thence into Greece, Notwithstanding the Opposition of all their Enemies*. Modern editions of the same classic have three- or four-word titles like *The March Upcountry* and *The Expedition of Cyrus*.

FIGURE 3.1 Title page of *The Workes of Benjamin Jonson*. London: William Stansby, 1616. Engraved by William Hole. Folger Shakespeare Library, STC 14751 copy 1.

Other early modern title pages, particularly those for more luxurious books, provided information about the contents in pictures rather than words. The engraved title page to *The Works of Benjamin Jonson*, published in 1616, offers a good example of a pictorial title page (fig. 3.1). Symbolic figures and scenes organized in and around a classical archway give readers a visual introduction to the contents of the book. Personifications of Tragedy and Comedy stand between columns on either side of the archway. Above it, figures representing Tragicomedy, Satire, and Pastoral Literature surround a Roman theater. Below the archway, a traveling players' wagon and a Greek amphitheater represent the roots of drama. This is the facade of the book, as it were, with the title inscribed front and center, as if serving as the doorway that a reader will pass through to reach the rest of the text.

Publishers John Heminge and Henry Condell would have looked to Jonson's *Works* when developing the First Folio, since Jonson's was, in 1623, the only other folio-sized collection of contemporary literature to include plays. The title page design they adopted, however, reverses the standard model that Jonson and others had used. Instead of placing the words front and center with a pictorial frame around them to summarize the book's contents, the author portrait indicates that this book does not just contain plays—rather, it is a monument to Shakespeare. The words that would normally be in the middle of an engraved title page are pushed out of the way to make room for a representation of the author—Mr. William Shakespeare himself.

Author portraits are not unusual today. They often appear on the back of a book, or the back flap of a hardcover's dustjacket. Editions of literary classics might even have the author's portrait on the front cover. In the early seventeenth century, though, author portraits were fairly rare. They sometimes appeared as small medallions integrated into the design surrounding the title page text, but

FIGURE 3.2   Frontispiece and title page of *The Workes of the Most High and Mightie Prince, James by the Grace of God King of Great Britain, France and Ireland*. London: Robert Barker and John Bill for James, Bishop of Winton, 1616. Frontispiece engraved by Simon de Pass, title page engraved by Renold Elstracke. Folger Shakespeare Library, STC 14344 copy 1.

FIGURE 3.3   Jan van der Straet, "Impressio librorum," from *Nova Reperta*. Antwerp: Philippe Galle, ca. 1591. Folger Shakespeare Library, ART Vol. f81 no.4.

more often they appeared on their own, as a large frontispiece image opposite the title page. The 1616 edition of King James's *Works* has a pictorial title page with an architectural frame similar to Ben Jonson's *Works* of the same year, but it also has a frontispiece with a large portrait of the king and four lines of verse praising him (fig. 3.2). Both the title page and the frontispiece are engravings, an intaglio (defined below) printing technique that is generally considered to have been a more opulent medium.

The compilers of Shakespeare's First Folio could have placed the author portrait in the usual location, on the frontispiece. Instead, they defied convention and placed the large portrait on the title page itself. Even more strangely, the title page combines relief and intaglio printing on the same sheet. Each technique requires a different kind of printing press, so each copy of the title page had to be printed in two separate steps and in two separate shops.

Normal book printing is a relief technique. That is, the parts that carry the ink stand up from the base of the surface in relief, like a modern rubber stamp (see fig. 4.2 and Claire M. L. Bourne's chapter on typography in this volume). After the raised surface is inked and paper laid on top, it takes relatively little pressure to transfer the ink to the paper using a common press. Jan van der Straet's "Impressio librorum" (The Printing of Books) from circa 1591 depicts an idealized version of this kind of print shop (fig. 3.3). On the left, seated typesetters pick out individual letters and spaces with their right hands, placing them upside down and backwards on the tray-like composing sticks held in their left hands, building up the text line by line. The man standing in the center background applies ink to the surface of the set type using leather pads covered in sticky black ink. In the right middle ground, a pressman pulls the lever that lowers the platen to put even pressure on the paper placed over the inked type.

Any combination of letters could be put together to create words. Blocks of pictorial or decorative elements cut in relief could likewise be set among the words. Because the letters and the pictures stood up in relief at the same height, they were inked and then passed under the platen at the same time. In the First Folio, nonverbal relief elements include the rectangular headpieces at the start of each play and the triangular tailpieces that filled in the blank space at the end of some plays. In theory, the portrait of Shakespeare on the title page could also have been cut into a woodblock and printed in relief at the same time as the text. This would have been the cheapest and easiest option for a pictorial title page.

Woodcut pictorial title pages for plays were not unheard of. A number of quarto editions of plays from the time (though none of Shakespeare's) have them.

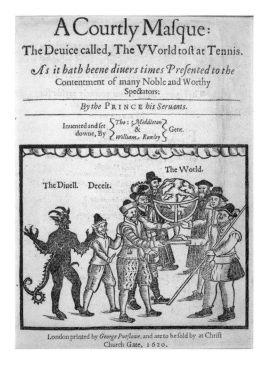

FIGURE 3.4 Woodcut title page of Thomas Middleton and William Rowley, *The World Tost at Tennis*. London: George Purslowe for Edward Wright, 1620. Folger Shakespeare Library, STC 17910.

For example, the court masque *The World Tost at Tennis* (1620) by Thomas Middleton and James Rowley reveals one of the drawbacks of woodcut illustrations (fig. 3.4). Note the relative lack of detail compared with the images seen so far in this chapter. White lines on a black background are easily lost in the texture of the wood grain. Black lines on a white background have to be fairly thick because they are created by cutting away the wood on either side. If the woodcutter left too thin a line, the wood would break, leaving unintended white space and gaps in the image.

The relative ease and inelegance of printing images from woodcuts argued against using a woodcut portrait on the title page of the First Folio. A woodcut could have branded the publication as a lesser genre of literature. Instead, the editors went with the more refined—and much slower and more expensive—option of an engraved portrait.

Engraving is an intaglio technique. The term *intaglio* comes from the Italian verb *intagliare*, meaning "to cut in." Intaglio printing is the inverse of a woodcut: the lines that print black are cut into the surface material, which is traditionally copper or a copper alloy. Preparing an engraved plate for printing involves heating it to make the cuts more receptive to the ink, then rubbing ink over the surface, being sure to force it fully into the cut lines. The surface of the plate must then be repeatedly and carefully wiped to fully remove excess ink lying on top of the plate without also picking up the ink that has been forced into the cuts. Because the ink is held in the recesses below the plate's surface, it takes great pressure to transfer ink to paper—literally requiring the paper to be forced into the cut lines to take up the ink. This is more pressure than a common press can provide. Intaglio printing therefore requires a rolling press, as shown in another idealized scene by Jan van der Straet from circa 1591, "Sculptura in Aes" (Engraving in Copper) (fig. 3.5).

To make an intaglio print, the inked and wiped plate is set face up on the bed of the press. Dampened paper is carefully positioned over the plate, then covered with soft blankets. A skilled pressman slowly and smoothly cranks the stack of blankets, paper, and copper plate between two closely spaced horizontal cylinders. Intense pressure from the cylinders through the blankets forces the dampened paper into the ink-filled recesses cut into the plate. When the printer peels the paper off the plate, the paper pulls the ink up with it, transferring the image from plate to paper. This slow process of inking, wiping, and cranking through the press had to be repeated for each copy pulled.

Evidence that an image is an intaglio print rather than a relief print comes not only from the greater detail of line that the medium affords, but also from the telltale impression left behind by the beveled edges of the metal plate. This

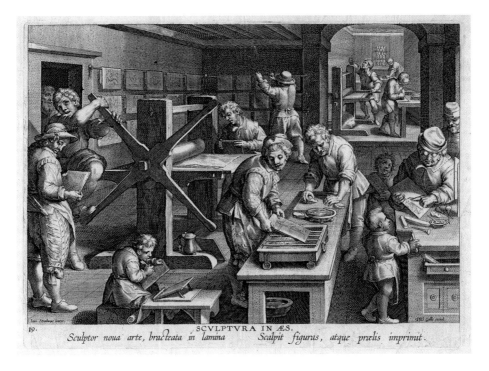

FIGURE 3.5   Jan van der Straet, "Sculptura in aes," from *Nova Reperta*. Antwerp: Philippe Galle, ca. 1591. Folger Shakespeare Library, ART Vol. f81 no.19.

"plate mark" often has traces of ink on the edges, making it even easier to detect, as in the Ben Jonson title page seen in figure 3.1. Notice how the Ben Jonson plate mark is only slightly larger than the printed image: being expensive, every last bit of the copper plate's surface was put to use. The large engraved plates used to print the frontispiece and title page of King James's *Works* in figure 3.2 are likewise engraved almost to the edges, and would have been similarly expensive.

If you compare the size of the plate mark on the title page of the First Folio to the size of the page as a whole, it's clear that the copper plate was considerably smaller than would be expected (fig. 3.6). Measuring seven and three-quarters by six and a quarter inches, it is only about half as big as the copper plates normally used to print title pages of comparable size. Like the Ben Jonson and King James examples, the engraved design extends nearly to the edges of the plate, but this time the only text on the plate is the artist's credit line, "Martin Droeshout sculpsit, London" (the Latin term *sculpsit*, meaning "engraved by," commonly identified the printmaker in the early modern period). The remainder of the title page text is printed from moveable type, in relief. This composite layout would have allowed for the use of a smaller sheet of copper for the engraved portrait,

FIGURE 3.6 Title page of the First Folio with the Droeshout portrait in its first state. Folger Shakespeare Library, STC 22273 Fo.1 no.02.

but it also meant that each copy of the title page had to be run through two presses: a common press for the type, and a rolling press for the engraving.

In practice, such hybrid work was done by printing the typographic content first, leaving a blank space for the engraving. Those preprinted sheets would then be taken to a separate intaglio shop, where the engraved image would be added using a rolling press. The challenge of precisely lining up (or "registering") the two stages of printing means that pages with both relief and intaglio printing sometimes have a slightly crooked aspect. The engraved image might even overlap the printed text in some cases. Occasionally (though not with any known copies of the Shakespeare Folios) the sheet was put through the rolling press backward, rendering the engraved image upside down. Given that paper and copper were comparatively expensive, less-than-perfect examples still made it to market. Indeed, the relative cost of copper compared to labor points to a likely reason for the hybrid title page: an engraved folio-sized title page signals an important book, but if such a large investment in copper was not possible, the effect could be approximated by combining a half-sized copper plate with moveable type. The extra time and labor involved in printing the same sheet on two presses would cost less than doubling the amount of copper and the amount of work required of the engraver.

Because of the attribution in the lower left corner of the plate, we know that Martin Droeshout engraved the portrait, but which Martin Droeshout? Two men by that name lived and worked in London's immigrant community of artists from the Low Countries—so-called Martin Droeshout the Elder, born in Brussels in 1573/74, and that man's nephew, Martin Droeshout the Younger, born in London in 1601. The Shakespeare portrait is one of three known Martin Droeshout engravings from 1623, his earliest securely datable works. One of these, a large allegory of "Spirituall warfare invented by Richard Cotes and graven by Martin Droset" is listed as such in the Stationers' Register, a record of publication privileges that was mostly limited to printed texts and not standalone engravings. Relatively few engravings were entered into the Register, and even fewer had named artists associated with them. It would seem that Martin Droeshout was someone worth mentioning. Martin the Younger was only twenty-two at the time. Twenty-two seems young today, but it wasn't so young in an era when children began apprenticeships by their early teens. Martin Droeshout the Younger's more famous contemporary, Simon de Passe, was producing sought-after engravings from the age of seventeen. Moreover, by 1623, the elder Martin was forty-nine or fifty, an unlikely age for the appearance of one's first dated engravings.

Additional evidence that the engraver was the younger of the two Martin Droeshouts comes from his later career. It was long thought that Martin

Droeshout ceased engraving in 1632, and therefore died around then, but in fact, he moved to Spain and continued engraving until at least 1639 (Schuckman 1991). His Spanish engravings had previously escaped notice due to the fact that he signed them "Droeswood" rather than Droeshout—"hout" being Dutch for wood or timber. Anglicizing half of his name no doubt eased Droeshout's career in Catholic Spain by putting as much distance as possible between him and his Dutch Protestant ancestry. That Martin Droeshout worked in a deeply Catholic environment also supports the idea that the engraver was Martin the Younger rather than Martin the Elder. Not only was Martin the Elder known to have been present in London on several occasions during the period that "Martin Droeswood en Madrid" signatures appeared, records show that he was an active member of the Austin Friars' Dutch Reformed Church in London, whereas his nephew is unmentioned after his infant baptism (Schlueter 2007). While it is possible that the engraver moved back and forth between Spain and England during those years, and possible that financial motives compelled a devout Protestant to engrave pictures of Catholic saints and Counter-Reformation symbolism, it is unlikely.

The *Spiritual Warfare* engraving cited in the Stationers' Register is inscribed "Ric: Cotes inuentor" and "MDhout sculpsit" within the plate, matching the register's statement that Cotes was responsible for the design and Droeshout translated that design into an engraving. In contrast, the First Folio portrait only has a "sculpsit" statement. There is no mention of the original artist behind the design. Because the "inventor" of the design is not named, the artist's identity was either unknown to the publishers or of no marketable value. It is possible that the original design showed just the head and neck area—not an uncommon composition at the time. This would account for the proportional mismatch between the head and the too-small body, which Droeshout would have grafted on from another composition.

The Droeshout engraving exists in four different states, but those four states do not correspond to the First, Second, Third, and Fourth Folios (fig. 3.7). The term "state" has a slightly different meaning in intaglio printing than it does in printing from moveable type. For book historians, "state" and "edition" both refer to differences in the setting of type, but to different degrees. A single edition of a book is printed from more or less the same setting of moveable type in more or less the same printing campaign. Minor differences in typesetting within a single edition, such as stop-press corrections to fix printer's errors, result in different "states" of a given sheet. Differences in state are not meant to be noticed by ordinary readers. Different editions, on the other hand, are signaled by different publication information on the title page. When the contents have changed significantly (or even insignificantly, as when a "new edition" is simply a marketing ploy), publishers often call attention to that fact. In contrast, any change to an engraved plate, no matter how small, results in a new state.

The first state of the Droeshout portrait of Shakespeare, shown here in figure 3.6, is the most awkward looking of the four. Shakespeare's head appears to have been cut out of one picture and superimposed onto another. It seems to float over the large white collar. Only four impressions from the first state of the plate are known to exist, one in London at the British Library, one in Oxford at the Bodleian Library, and two in Washington, DC, at the Folger Shakespeare Library. In other words, it is very rare. The people funding the publication evidently thought that it was unsatisfactory enough to send the plate back to the engraver for improvement, but not so unsatisfactory that the earliest impressions needed to be scrapped. What's more, the text at the top and bottom of the title page would have already been printed on a common press, so as well as wasting paper, throwing away impressions of the engraving meant throwing away perfectly good printing.

In the second state of the engraving, Martin Droeshout added diagonal lines to the area of the collar below Shakespeare's left ear, using crosshatching to create the illusion of a shadow cast by his head. This made the portrait look more like an image of a real person. He also gave Shakespeare considerably more stubble, presumably making the portrait look more like Shakespeare's friends and colleagues remembered him. The plate went back to the printing house, and step two of producing the First Folio's title page resumed for a time. At some point, though, production stopped again so that the plate could be reworked some more. It had not worn out or suffered damage, so it did not technically need reworking; Heminge and Condell must simply have wanted it improved.

The changes made in the third state of the engraving are so minor that they are barely noticeable. Each of the diamond-shaped highlights glinting in Shakespeare's pupils was modified with a horizontal line to reduce its brightness and, arguably, make the eyes more lifelike. The other change makes Shakespeare's hair slightly more lifelike: a single strand of hair stands out of place on the right, breaking the rigid outer edge of his severely coiffed head. To find it, imagine a clock face centered on Shakespeare's nostril. The strand of hair is between one o'clock and two o'clock. Once again, the touched-up plate was returned to production, and the remaining copies of the First Folio's title page went through the rolling press with the plate in this third state. The plate stayed in good condition for decades, so all copies of the Second and Third Folios also have the Droeshout portrait in the third state. The plate was not reworked again until it came time to print the Fourth Folio, when an unknown engraver cut additional lines into

FIGURE 3.7 Details from the first, second, third, and fourth states of the Droeshout portrait. Folger Shakespeare Library, ART Box D783 no.1, STC 22273 Fo.1 no.01, STC 22273 Fo.1 no.68, and S2915 Fo.4 no.01.

the face, hair, and clothing to strengthen the crosshatching so that the worn-down plate could hold more ink, keeping it from looking too pale. This fourth and final state is the plate's last known use.

Adding a shadow on Shakespeare's collar undoubtedly improved the portrait, but not by much. The other changes are so minor that they hardly seem worth the trouble. Was this the best that Martin Droeshout could manage? Looking at some of his other engravings shows that, in fact, he could do better. Droeshout's portrait of James Marquis of Hamilton is dated 1623, the same year as the First Folio, and was printed from a similarly-sized piece of copper. Instead of just head and shoulders, it depicts Hamilton as a richly dressed full-length figure. He stands on a patterned floor with his left hand resting next to a plumed helmet on a silk-draped table. Swags of fabric hang on either side of him, providing visual interest. It is no masterpiece, but Droeshout's attention to detail here far surpasses the simple depiction of Shakespeare. Similarly, Droeshout's engraved title page for *The Prophecies of the Twelve Sybills* squeezes even more detail onto a smaller copper plate, just under four and a half inches wide (fig. 3.8). It also provides another example of a fully engraved title page, a reminder that the title page of the First Folio could have been fully engraved, but wasn't. Although it is undated, *The Prophecies* would have been produced some time between 1620 and 1625 based on the publisher's address "at the Angell in Lumbard Streete" during those years.

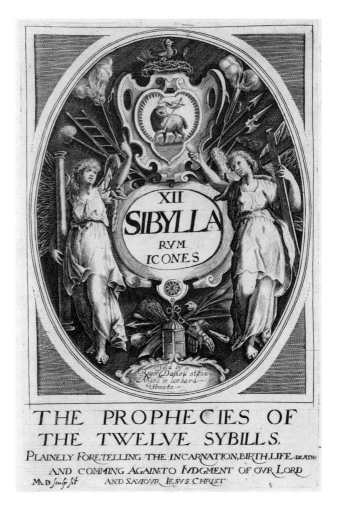

FIGURE 3.8   Title page of *The Prophecies of the Twelve Sybills*. London: Roger Daniel, ca. 1620–25. Engraved by Martin Droeshout. Folger Shakespeare Library, STC 22527a.5.

We don't have surviving documentation that shows the cost to produce the title page of the First Folio, but putting the clues together certainly makes it seem as though John Heminge and Henry Condell wanted something grander than they could afford. The most luxurious books had both an engraved frontispiece and an engraved title page. If this proved too expensive, an engraved title page alone, costing half as much as a pair of engravings, would still have been something special. Heminge and Condell halved the price of material one more time, though: they commissioned an engraving that was only half the size of the page. The young artist they chose, Martin Droeshout, had begun to make a name for himself, though not (we assume) to such an extent that his commissioners would have paid extra for the privilege.

The progressive changes to the plate between states one and three also hint at the publishers' stymied desire for more. We know that Martin Droeshout was capable of producing an engraving with a full-length figure, background details, and various props appropriate to a playwright, such as a desk, pen, and paper. So why didn't he? In addition to using more expensive material (copper versus wood), engraving is a more skilled and more labor-intensive process than woodcutting, so it is easy to imagine Droeshout stripping away the options to reach an acceptable price. Instead of placing the figure in an illusionistic three-dimensional space, the background could be a uniform flat gray made up of straight lines. With a bit more time and effort (and money), the background could be made more dynamic by having the parallel diagonal lines going in both directions on one side of the picture instead of just from upper right to lower left. This option shows in the finished print, where the left background is slightly darker than the right. Could the portrait have had an elaborate scrollwork frame engraved around it? Or perhaps be placed in a decorative oval? Yes, that could have been done, but it would have increased the price. The initial result, seen in the engraving's first state, must have been worse than its commissioners expected. The second state of the engraving corrected the missing shadow and chin stubble, but that evidently was not good enough, because a second round of touch-ups followed. This is speculation, but given that the only differences between the second and third states are the addition of one strand of hair and a horizontal line in each pupil's highlight, it looks suspiciously like Droeshout did the bare minimum required in order to be able to answer in the affirmative if someone asked whether the portrait had been improved.

Another piece of evidence that Heminge and Condell had originally envisioned something grander for the portrait comes from Ben Jonson's poem printed in moveable type on the page that faces the title page (fig. 3.9):

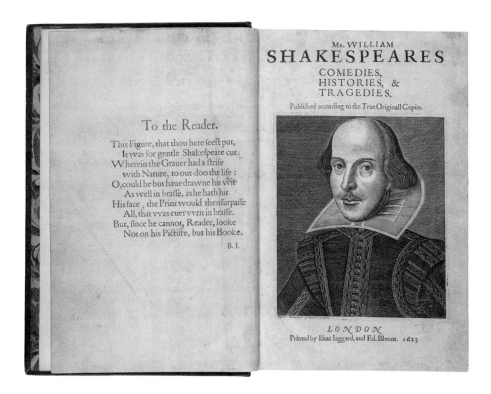

FIGURE 3.9 Frontispiece and title page of the First Folio with the Droeshout portrait in its third state. Folger Shakespeare Library, STC 22273 Fo.1 no.68.

> This Figure, that thou here seest put,
> It was for gentle Shakespeare cut;
> Wherein the Grauer had a strife
> with Nature, to out-doo the life:
> O, could he but haue drawne his wit
> As well in brasse, as he hath hit
> His face; the Print would then surpasse
> All, that was ever writ in brasse.
> But, since he cannot, Reader, looke
> Not on his Picture, but his Booke.

The length, style, and theme of Jonson's verse are akin to what one would expect to find written in the lower margin of an engraved portrait, and a frontispiece portrait in particular. If Heminge and Condell had hoped to publish a folio edition of Shakespeare's works on the grand model of the 1616 edition of King James's *Works* and similar publications, an engraved version of Ben Jonson's lines

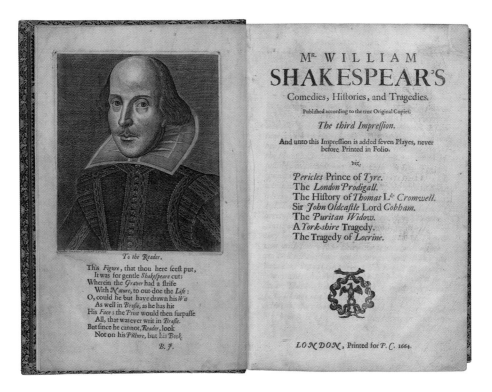

FIGURE 3.10   Frontispiece and title page of the 1664 Third Folio with the Droeshout portrait in its third state. Folger Shakespeare Library, S2914 Fo.3 no.18.

would have fit into the space below a conventional engraved frontispiece portrait. Placing the engraved author portrait on the title page instead of the frontispiece posed a problem for the poem, because laudatory verses only make sense when they're read alongside the portrait to which they refer: keeping them in the conventional position below the portrait would not be appropriate for a title page, and moving the lines elsewhere in the preliminaries would not be appropriate for the poem. The only option left was to have them printed alone, facing the portrait.

When the Second Folio appeared in 1632, the relationship between poem, portrait, and title page remained the same as in the First Folio: the portrait appears on the title page and Jonson's poem faces it. The only obvious differences are the addition of "The second Impression" above the portrait, and changes in the printers' names and the date in the imprint. At first, the Third Folio did the same, except with "The Third Impression" printed above the portrait and "Printed for Philip Chetwinde, 1663" added to the imprint. Then things changed. In 1664, a new title page and frontispiece were printed that reconfigured the established pattern of the Shakespeare Folios (fig. 3.10). Except for a small woodcut printer's device near the bottom, the 1664 version of the Third Folio title page is entirely filled with text. The poem no longer dominates the frontispiece; instead of large type and generous line spacing, it has been reduced to fit into the lower third of the page in order to make room for the Droeshout portrait above it. Moving the Droeshout portrait from the title page to the facing frontispiece for the 1664 printing created space to tout this edition's special feature—"unto this Impression is added seven Playes, never before Printed in Folio," followed by a list of seven new titles. Of the seven, only *Pericles* is still attributed to William Shakespeare, but the Third Folio was less concerned with scholarly accuracy than with convincing people they needed to buy the book. Even if you already owned a First or Second Folio, you would not have these seven plays. Oxford University's Bodleian Library famously decided that acquiring the newly expanded 1664 edition meant they no longer needed to keep their copy of the 1623 First Folio. The reverence for Shakespeare that developed from the middle of the eighteenth century did not yet exist. The First Folio was just an outdated book, so selling it as surplus material made sense. Amazingly, the Bodleian was able to buy back that copy when it resurfaced in the early twentieth century (see Zachary Lesser's chapter in this volume). The Fourth Folio, published in 1685, continued this new arrangement of the portrait and verses on the left side of the opening and the title page with printer's device on the right. The title page even included the exact same marketing ploy—"Unto which is added, Seven Plays Never before Printed in Folio"—despite the fact that the printing of these additional plays to accompany the 1664 issue of the Third Folio made the statement untrue.

Moving the Droeshout portrait of Shakespeare from the title page to the frontispiece part way through the printing of the Third Folio (and keeping it there for the Fourth Folio) not only made room for more words on the title page but also rectified a visual oddity that dated back to 1623. For the first time, readers opening Shakespeare's collected plays saw something that met contemporary expectations: an author portrait above a few lines of laudatory verse facing a title page that gave a verbal description of the book's contents. In a sense, this normalization formalized the assimilation of William Shakespeare's plays into the literary canon. Instead of looking unusual next to other important books, a Shakespeare Folio now belonged with them. What the publishers couldn't have predicted was that this normalcy would itself come to seem odd thanks to the bardolatry that began developing in the mid-eighteenth century. Today, the First Folio, Second Folio, and earlier printings of the Third Folio look as expected. It's later printings of the Third Folio and all printings of the Fourth that have the familiar portrait in the "wrong" place and a startlingly plain title page.

CHAPTER 4

"Folio" and Format
Supersizing Shakespeare

Tara L. Lyons

In 2023, as we celebrate the four-hundredth anniversary of Shakespeare's First Folio, it might be difficult to imagine that anyone in Shakespeare's time was unhappy that it had come to press. The puritan polemicist William Prynne, however, was one such person. In his anti-theatrical treatise, *Histrio-mastix: The Players Scourge* (1633), Prynne found the spiritual health of England's people in a deplorable state. He lamented that swarms of Londoners packed themselves into bawdy playhouses in lieu of attending church services, and rather than reading wholesome sermons, customers were buying seedy playbooks. Their sinful appetites for plays and relentless overconsumption were only encouraged, Prynne argued, by the greed of booksellers who were issuing playbooks in the tens of thousands. He observed that even the size of playbooks had increased: "Some Play-books . . . are growne from Quarto into Folio, which yet beare so good a price and sale, that I cannot but with griefe relate it" (1633, sig. **6v). Shakespeare Folios, or "Shackspeers Plaies" as Prynne called them, were a case in point, not just because they had "growne" in size, but also because they were "printed in the best Crowne paper, far better than most Bibles" (1633, sig. **6v). For Prynne, when plays demanded higher quality materials than God's own word and Christian souls were lacking in spiritual food, the last thing England needed were supersized portions of Shakespeare.

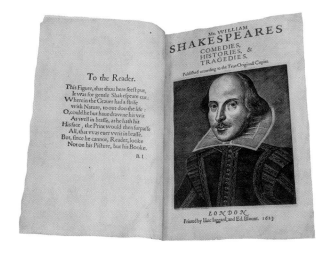

FIGURE 4.1 *Top*: Title page of the First Folio. The Rare Book & Manuscript Library, University of Illinois at Urbana-Champaign, IUQ00001. *Bottom*: Title page of Shakespeare's *The Merry Wives of Windsor* (1619). The Rare Book & Manuscript Library, University of Illinois at Urbana-Champaign, 822.33 P51619.

Of course, "supersized" was not a term that Prynne or his contemporaries applied to Shakespeare or his Folios. Rather, the word entered common American parlance when fast-food chains upsized their packaging for fries and soft drinks as part of a series of late-twentieth century marketing campaigns. Customers who wanted a size larger than "large" were encouraged to "supersize" their orders. Paying a slightly higher price bought them more food, and for the vendors, the additional costs for these larger portions were easy to offset, thereby increasing their profits. Cultural critics, reminiscent of Prynne, were quick to point out how flashy marketing for supersized portions were contributing to a health crisis. Juxtaposing a folio of plays of one of the most revered authors in the English language to supersized orders of fries and drinks might strike some as irreverent, but the comparison helps to contextualize Shakespeare's Folios as trendy commodities made, marketed, and consumed in the seventeenth century. Publishers found ways to make Shakespeare's books bigger—increasing their size and bulk and offering more plays in supersized textual containers—while still creating products that were profitable and enticing to customers who had many other options for buying plays. By focusing here on the production and marketing of the four Folios, I consider how booksellers responded and contributed to a desire for "more" and "bigger" books of Shakespeare, an appetite that has perhaps never quite been satiated.

FIRST FOLIO (1623)

As figure 4.1 shows, a copy of Shakespeare's *Merry Wives of Windsor* (1619) in quarto was little more than half the size of the First Folio (1623). When Prynne complained that these plays had "growne" in size, he was right. Not all folios were large books, however. "Folio" technically refers to a book created by folding sheets of paper in half along the long side, with each so-folded sheet of paper yielding two leaves or four pages (Gaskell 1995, 81). A "quarto" was created by folding a sheet of paper in half twice, thus creating four leaves or eight pages. Depending on the size of the paper, one could (in theory) have a quarto and folio that were the same size. Moreover, different sizes of paper could be used for the same book. For instance, some authors such as Ben Jonson arranged to have a few presentation copies of their folios printed on larger, higher quality paper (Gants and Lockwood 2014, 4). For the First Folio, formally entitled *Mr. William Shakespeares Comedies, Histories, & Tragedies* (1623), middle-grade "crown" paper was selected for the project (the names of seventeenth-century paper stock reflected the watermarks traditionally used to mark and identify each size, in this case an image of a crown). The dimensions of each sheet of unfolded crown paper were approximately thirteen and three-quarters in height by eighteen inches in width; when folded once, the sheet's two leaves were each approximately thirteen and three-quarters in height by nine inches in width. But the size of these leaves was then altered during the binding process. The three outer edges of the text block were trimmed by binders to remove ragged or uneven edges, sometimes removing a quarter to half an inch (or more) of a book's outer margins. Each time a book was rebound it was subject to further trimming, meaning that copies of the First Folio can sometimes vary more than an inch in leaf height and width. Differences can also be observed in the thickness of copies. During the binding process, binders would beat the pages of the book to compress the text block (Gaskell 1995, 147–8). In effect, some copies of the Folio will appear bulkier than others even though they contain the same number of leaves.

When Prynne commented on the growth of Shakespeare's plays, he was also concerned by the increasing cultural authority granted to playwrights in early modern England. For Prynne, the folio was a format properly reserved for writers of much greater importance and severity. England had seen a handful of its literary authors published in the folio format before 1623, including Geoffrey Chaucer, Sir Philip Sidney, Edmund Spenser, Samuel Daniel, and Ben Jonson. Nevertheless, Shakespeare was an unusual choice for folio publication in 1623, in part because the volume focused exclusively on his authorship of stage plays, leaving out his poetry. English plays from the London commercial theaters had been earning more respect as literary texts in the early seventeenth century, but not everyone was persuaded that plays from the professional stage were deserving of collected editions in their own right. When the *Works* of Ben Jonson was published in the folio format in 1616, for instance, its inclusion of nine stage plays incited derision from his critics, who mockingly inquired, "Pray tell me Ben, where doth the mystery lurk, / What others call a play you call a work?" (1640, sig. G3v). As if serving fast food on a silver platter, or soda in a crystal flute, Jonson was charged with packaging plays as luxury items, or "works" of intellectual and creative labor, when others considered them "plays"—recreational products for mass consumption derived from the entertainment industry. The publishers of Shakespeare's First Folio, however, seemed undeterred by such skeptics.

Present-day audiences frequently look upon Shakespeare's First Folio as one of the great cultural treasures of the West, yet it bears remembering that the Folio was also a commodity for sale in the English book trade. Prynne blamed the booksellers for contributing to the public's overconsumption of plays, but from another perspective, these men and women were merely astute professionals who sought ways to expand their profits by developing innovative products. Shakespeare's collected plays was one of these products, and in 1623, we find publishers experimenting with the folio format not only as packaging that conveyed prestige, but also as a medium that could efficiently and economically deliver a large number of playtexts to readers. Thirty-six plays were contained in the Shakespeare First Folio, making it the largest collection of English plays printed at that time. It seems, then, that Shakespeare's plays were "supersized" in 1623 because members of the book trade believed they could make more money by selling plays in larger portions.

The First Folio was a relatively expensive book to produce for its publishers. Before they could begin to recoup their investment through book sales, they needed to first invest capital in paper, the rights to print titles, and the labor and material costs associated with presswork. The cost of paper represented approximately 30 percent of the production budget for the Folio, and it might have been more if the publishers had chosen a different format (Bidwell 2008, 590). The First Folio is 908 pages, representing 227 individual sheets of paper. Had the

FIGURE 4.2 The First Folio, p. 391 (leaf 3b2r). Carnegie Mellon University Libraries, Special Collections, PR2751 .A4 1623.

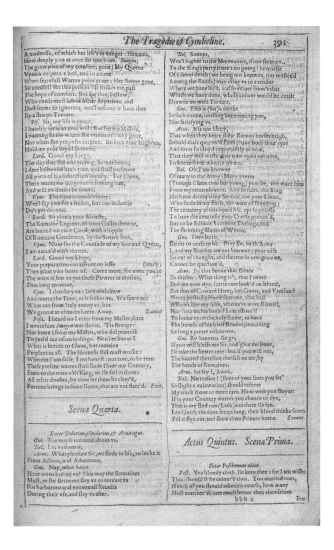

publishers chosen to publish all thirty-six plays in quarto (one fold and format smaller), Steven K. Galbraith estimates that the project would have required a full 352 sheets of paper (2010, 65). Thus, as Galbraith reminds us, the Shakespeare Folio "is a folio . . . because it did not make sense to print it in any other format" (2010, 66). It was simply cheaper to produce in folio. Comparing the cost of paper for the Jonson folio makes this point clear. For the nine Jonson plays in his *Works* (1616), 172 sheets of paper were required. In quarto, those same nine plays required just under 106 sheets. Therefore, Jonson's plays would have been less costly to produce in quarto (Galbraith 2010, 61–63). That publishers chose the more expensive option for Jonson's folio tells us that the *Works* (1616) was designed to look like a luxury product with large margins and ample white space on each page. Shakespeare's Folio, in contrast, was more economically produced.

Other features of the First Folio reveal how its publishers sought to cut costs on the project. As one can see in figure 4.2., Shakespeare's plays were set in two columns on each page. The margins around the text were not lavishly spaced, meaning that most of the page was devoted to the display of text. When compared to a page from Jonson's folio (fig. 4.3), one sees immediately how much more crowded Shakespeare's Folio was. The type used in the First Folio—a so-called "pica" roman, one line of which measures approximately 4 mm in height (see Claire M. L. Bourne's chapter in this volume)—was also smaller than the type used in Jonson's 1616 *Works*, meaning that any one line of Shakespeare's text could accommodate more characters (Gaskell 1995, 15). And Shakespeare's Folio did fit far more lines onto a page compared with Jonson's. The Shakespeare Folio was also larger, and in particular taller, than Jonson's, a consequence of the different sizes of paper employed for each project. As mentioned above, Shakespeare's Folio was produced on crown paper, creating pages that were roughly thirteen and three-eighths inches in height by eight and a half inches in width after binding. Jonson's folio was produced on "pot" paper that was typically smaller than crown paper, producing pages that measure approximately eleven and three-quarters in height by seven and a quarter inches in width. While the choice of crown paper for the Shakespeare project might seem unusual in that it was the more expensive choice, the larger sheet size provided a taller page (almost two inches compared to pot paper), allowing the printers to fit more of Shakespeare onto each page (Galbraith 2010, 64–5).

Of course, if the publishers of Shakespeare's Folio were seeking ways to cut costs, they could have reduced the number of plays in the volume. That sacrifice, however, was not one the publishers were willing to make. In fact, even after the initial volume was printed, the publishers decided to squeeze one late addition into the Folio that had been delayed on account of a dispute with its rights holder. Shakespeare's *Troilus and Cressida* was not part of the original Folio printing—the title does not appear in the "Catalogue of Plays" (i.e., the table of contents) at the start of the volume, and the play's text is somewhat awkwardly inserted into the volume between the "histories" and "tragedies," where there is a break in pagination (Blayney 1991, 21–23). Still, the late addition of *Troilus and Cressida* demonstrates the publishers' priorities in producing the volume: more Shakespeare was better, even if the Catalogue did not reflect the volume's contents, and even if it meant breaking the work's neat generic divisions (i.e., comedies followed by histories and tragedies).

If the publishers of Shakespeare's Folio aimed to offer customers a product unlike anything else on the market, the book needed to do something new with printed plays. What the publishers came up with was actually quite novel for

FIGURE 4.3 Jonson's *Works* (1616), p. 211 (leaf S4r). The Rare Book & Manuscript Library, University of Illinois at Urbana-Champaign, Q. 822 J731616.

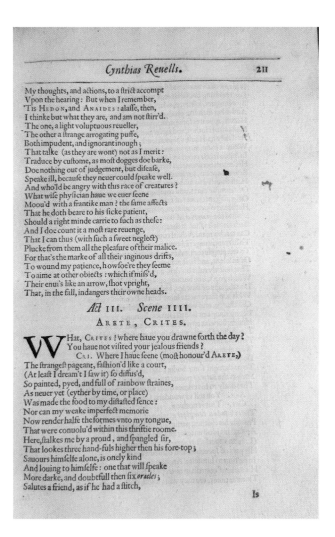

the time. They took a mass of plays by one author and sold them all together in one volume. In fact, even before the Folio project was completed, the single folio volume was advertised to potential buyers as a feature. In 1622, the Shakespeare Folio was advertised in John Bill's bookseller's catalogue as "Playes, written by M. William Shakespeare, *all in one volume,* printed by Isaack Iaggard, in fol" (Greg 1962, 1109, emphasis added). The phrase "all in one volume" did not have a static or stable meaning in the book trade, but in this case, it meant that all of the plays would be sold together under a joint title in one integral edition, and not as separate published books that could then be assembled into one.

That the Shakespeare Folio was sold in "one volume" may not seem like an innovation, but when placed against the other available options, it was. The most common format for English printed plays was quarto. As noted above, printing all thirty-six plays in quarto would have resulted in a volume that was bulky and unwieldy. Technically, it could have been made and even bound, but the publishers more than likely suspected that customers would be less willing to buy a super-thick quarto of plays. Alternatively, the collection could have been divided into an attractive two-volume or even three-volume quarto set, the volumes divided by genre (comedies and tragedies; or comedies, histories, and tragedies). Plenty of other books appeared in multiple volumes at the time, but the Folio's publishers must have reasoned that the extra costs in paper to produce the collection in quarto would not be easy to recover. Speculating on what readers would spend their money on, Blount and the Jaggards bet instead on a single volume in folio.

Crucially, the contents within that volume had been preassembled for the reader. Selling an author's works in "one volume" could have different meanings in the seventeenth century. Comparing the Shakespeare Folio with the two folio editions of Edmund Spenser's works, published in 1611 and 1617, is instructive on this point. All three folios were marketed as collections in "one volume," but each was different in composition. For the publishers of Spenser's folio in 1611, the words "one volume" appeared on the newly printed title page advertising *The faerie queen: The shepheards calendar: together with the other works of England's arch-poet, Edm. Spenser: collected into one volume, and carefully corrected*. This folio of Spenser's "works" consisted of a shrewdly marketed gathering of separately printed books—unsold copies of *The Faerie Queene* printed in 1609 joined with *The Shepheardes Calendar* (1611) and *Colin Clout* (1611). The 1617 edition of Spenser's "works" represented a similar gathering of independently printed titles that were issued together with a newly printed title page. As Jeffrey Todd Knight explains, "rather than issuing from the press as an integral book, it appeared in multiple printed productions, each with its own title page, to be bound together as—or if—the reader desired" (2013, 168). Spenser's folio was a kind of "build-it-yourself" volume, allowing flexibility in contents and the order of titles (Galbraith 2006, 21–2). By contrast, the Shakespeare Folio allowed the reader to avoid this labor of compiling its contents.

The First Folio's makeup is best understood in the context of the variety of options available to buyers and readers of books in the seventeenth century. By choosing to sell Shakespeare's plays in one volume, the publishers were speculating that readers would be more likely to buy all thirty-six plays compared to plays issued as independent parts. The publishers' assumptions about what readers wanted may have stemmed from the sales of Shakespeare's plays prior to 1623. When the First Folio was published, it added eighteen newly printed plays to Shakespeare's canon; the remaining eighteen plays had previously appeared in the quarto or octavo format. If readers wanted all eighteen of Shakespeare's plays available in print up to 1623, they would need to go hunting for them in bookshops, and if they could find them, collect them together and have them bound as a set. Or they might have hired a bookseller to do the searching and compiling for them. We do know that readers and collectors in the period were buying up playbooks and creating their own multi-play volumes (Pratt 2015, 321–27; August 2022, 16–17). For instance, Sir John Harington collected English plays from the theaters before 1611 and had them bound in custom made "tomes." But little evidence suggests that readers were homing in on Shakespeare as an organizing principle for their bespoke play collections. This could have changed after 1619.

Customers shopping for playbooks in 1619 might have come across these ten Shakespeare plays sold both as independent playbooks and as a preassembled set that was sewn or bound together: *The Whole Contention Between the Two Famous Houses Lancaster and York* (combining *Henry the Sixth, Part 2* and *Part 3*); *A Midsummer Night's Dream*; *1 Sir John Oldcastle*; *The Merchant of Venice*; *Henry the Fifth*; *King Lear*; *Pericles*; *The Merry Wives of Windsor*; and *A Yorkshire Tragedy*. This publishing project has often been called the Pavier Quartos, as the imprint on five of the title pages identified "T. P." or Thomas Pavier as the publisher. Yet, all of the quartos were printed by William Jaggard, and evidence suggests that the assembled playbooks that were sold from Jaggard's shop included his publication of Thomas Heywood's *A Woman Killed with Kindness* (1617) (Knight 2013, 69–70; Lesser 2021, 52–53). (Below, I refer to the project as the 1619 Quartos because there is no definitive evidence proving that either Pavier or Jaggard was the prime mover for the collection.) All but *Henry the Fifth* announced Shakespeare's authorship on their title pages, so that when compiled together, the volume became the first publisher's collection of plays attributed to Shakespeare. Moreover, modern scholars have determined that *1 Sir John Oldcastle* and *A Yorkshire Tragedy* may have been associated with Shakespeare or his playing company but they were not written by him (Kirwan 2015, 216-217). Hence, when customers bought the 1619 Quartos collection, they were buying a volume that was mostly, but not entirely, devoted to the plays of William Shakespeare.

Like the First Folio, the 1619 Quartos collection compiled plays into "one volume," but the publishers did little else to make the set look or feel like a uniform collection. There was no general title page or table of contents, no frontispiece with the author's portrait or commendatory verses. What made these volumes appear even more variegated were the imprint dates on the individual quartos' title pages. *The Whole Contention* was undated, but *Midsummer, Oldcastle*, and *Merchant* were falsely dated 1600, while *Henry the Fifth* and *King Lear* were falsely dated 1608. Although a newly printed collection, the 1619 Quartos were made to look like an assemblage of old and new playbooks that were not all

FIGURE 4.4 The Third Folio, title page. Carnegie Mellon University Libraries, Special Collections, PR2751 .A4 1663.

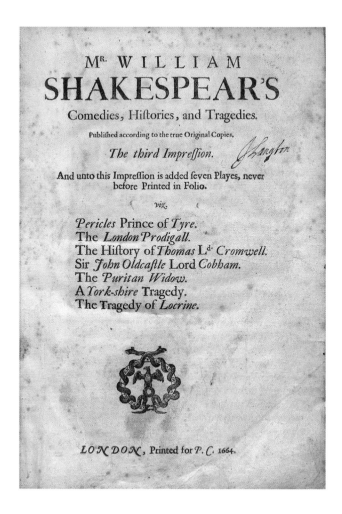

coming out of Jaggard's press at the same time. Critics have not come to a consensus about the publishers' motivations for the deceptive imprints, but what is clear is that booksellers were anticipating (or perhaps responding to) customers' desires to have plays collected into sets for them—old and new together, ten or more at a time. Successful sales of the 1619 Quartos would also have encouraged the Folio's publishers in 1623 to take the bigger risk.

By 1623, the First Folio offered more than three times this number of Shakespeare plays, organized by genre and neatly secured in "one volume," with additional aids to readers, such as the Catalogue that helped them navigate the 908-page edition.

The prefatory epistles and commendatory poems likewise assured readers that all thirty-six of the plays were authentically Shakespeare's and the project was a monument to Shakespeare. The curated First Folio promised readers a much fuller reading experience than any other Shakespeare product sold at the time.

THE SECOND FOLIO (1632)

Customers evidently were keen to buy the First Folio, as a second edition—the Second Folio—was published just nine years later in 1632, an event that likely incited Prynne's contempt for Shakespeare in 1633. The Second Folio was a page-for-page reprint of the First, using the same quality and amount of paper. While the 1632 volume did not change significantly in size or shape, the makers still thought their collection needed a minor upgrade. Thus, in addition to reprinting the prefatory verses from the First Folio, the second edition added three more commemorative poems that aggrandized the author and his works: "Upon the Effigies of my worth Friend, the Author Master William Shakespeare, and his Workes," "An Epitaph on the admirable Dramaticke Poet, W. Shakespeare," and "On Worthy Master Shakespeare and his Poems."

Together, these poems argued for the book's overwhelming capacity to memorialize the great author Shakespeare. The anonymous poet of "Upon the Effigies," for instance, reassures readers that the authentic Shakespeare would not be found by looking upon some effigy or image of the author; instead, they could experience the real Shakespeare within the pages of this book: *To see / The truer image, and a livelier he / Turne Reader* (¶5r). Similarly, another poem added to the Second Folio alludes to the volume as a repository for Shakespeare's living verse. The poet with the initials "J. M. S." contends that while the author's physical body has been destroyed by death, his lines live on in a new material form, the book, which is "a lesse volumne" (*2r) (meaning smaller than the author's mortal body), but readers would discover that it was overflowing with the genius of Shakespeare. A third additional poem, "An Epitaph," written by John Milton but appearing anonymously in the Second Folio, avows that the Folio is an enduring "monument" that will outlast even a "starre-ypointing Pyramid" (¶5r). These juxtapositions of the immortal book with effigies and grand funerary monuments reinforced to customers that the Folio was Shakespeare's own self-constructed monument, a compact textual tome (or tomb) to carry on the works of this larger-than-life author.

THE THIRD FOLIO (1663–1664)

The Third Folio of Shakespeare's plays was published in 1663 in a volume that looked remarkably similar to the First and Second Folios. But, in 1664, seven more plays were added to the Shakespearean canon and a new title page was printed to advertise the addition: *Pericles*; *The London Prodigal*; *The History of*

Thomas Lord Cromwell; *1 Sir John Oldcastle*; *The Puritan Widow*; *A Yorkshire Tragedy*; and *The Tragedy of Locrine* (fig. 4.4). To identify these supplemental titles, the publisher Philip Chetwind sought out playbooks previously attributed to Shakespeare or "W. S." on their title pages. Jaggard's 1619 Quartos—*Pericles*, *1 Sir John Oldcastle*, and *A Yorkshire Tragedy*—were reintroduced to the Shakespeare canon alongside the anonymous *The London Prodigal* (1605) and *The History of Thomas Lord Cromwell* (1602, 1613), and Thomas Middleton's *The Puritan Widow* (1607). Although of these seven plays, only *Pericles* is now accepted by scholars as having been cowritten by Shakespeare, the Third Folio's publisher seems to have been confident that adding more Shakespeare, apocryphal or not, was a sound marketing strategy (Kirwan 2015, 216).

The publication of seven additional plays in folio in the 1660s ensured that the reissued Third Folio was the most comprehensive volume of Shakespeare works in print (at 257 edition sheets compared to 227 for the First Folio) and that it thus superseded the preceding two Folios. In the meantime, between 1623 and 1664, twenty separate editions of Shakespeare's plays and poems were printed in quarto, indicating that there was still an appetite for Shakespeare's plays in smaller formats alongside the three supersized Folios (Murphy 2021, 394–400). Big Shakespeare was in fashion, but it was not the only Shakespeare for sale.

FOURTH FOLIO (1685)

In 1685, when the Fourth Folio of Shakespeare's *Comedies, Histories, and Tragedies* appeared in print, it was a stately book, taller than any of the Shakespeare editions before it. Trimmed pages of the Fourth Folio measure approximately fourteen and a half inches in height by nine and a half inches in width, and when compared to earlier editions like the First, there is no question that Shakespeare had been supersized again (fig. 4.5). Booksellers identified the Fourth Folio of his plays as a "large folio," signaling that even among folios, it was on the larger side. The added height of the Folio resulted from the use of "demy" paper, sheets of which measured approximately fifteen inches in height by nineteen and a half inches in width—this was one step up from the original crown (Bidwell 2008, 590). New mechanical developments after 1666 afforded printers the efficient use of larger sheets of paper on their presses (Pollard 1941, 130). Thus, the size of the Fourth Folio was both a choice on the part of the publishers who wanted to sell Shakespeare in "large folio" and a consequence of what was economically and mechanically possible in the late seventeenth century.

FIGURE 4.5   The Four Shakespeare Folios in sequence from left to right, showing the added height of each subsequent edition. The difference is most dramatic in the Fourth Folio of 1685, which seems to tower over the earlier Folios. Carnegie Mellon University Libraries, Special Collections, PR2751 .A4 1623, PR2751 .A4 1632, PR2751 .A4 1663, and PR2751 .A4 1685.

Since Shakespeare's corpus had grown by seven more plays in 1664, it makes sense that the publishers of the Fourth Folio would include these additions in their new and improved volume, though they erroneously (or perhaps intentionally) claimed on the 1685 title page that these plays had been "never before printed in folio" (fig. 4.6). As we've already seen, false advertising was not a rare event in the English book trade, but the reality was that in 1685, there may not have been many Third Folios with the seven-play supplement circulating. Scholars conjecture that a significant number of copies of these 1663/64 Folios were destroyed during the Great Fire of London in 1666. Less than twenty years later, when the Fourth Folio was published, the book was likely the best chance readers had to acquire all forty-three of Shakespeare plays (Depledge 2018, 157). And presumably early modern customers were counting.

When the London booksellers Richard Bentley and James Magnes listed the Fourth Folio in a catalogue of books for sale in their shop in 1686, they included the number of plays in the Folio in their marketing description: "Mr. *Shakespear*'s Plays: in one large Fol. Volume. Containing 43 Plays" ("Some Books printed," 1686). The number "43" was not advertised anywhere in the Fourth

FIGURE 4.6 The Fourth Folio, title page. Carnegie Mellon University Libraries, Special Collections, PR2751 .A4 1685.

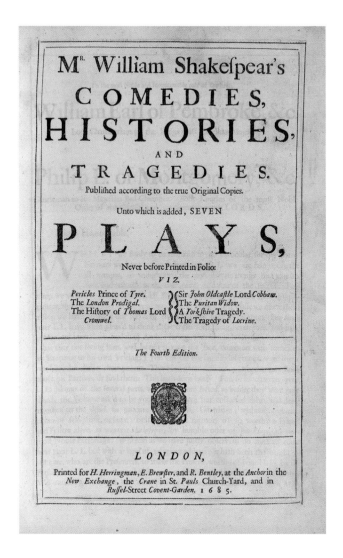

Folio, so this appears to have been the booksellers' own scheme for marketing the volume. In doing so, Bentley and Magnes established "43" as the number of dramatic texts that comprised Shakespeare's complete dramatic canon, a number that would allow Shakespeare enthusiasts to identify for themselves what was missing from their libraries.

For readers who were more interested in reading old plays than plays specifically written by Shakespeare, the Fourth Folio was also a trove of pre-Restoration texts. Like the other Folios, Shakespeare's name received priority at the top of the title page, but in 1685, the word "PLAYS" took center stage (fig. 4.6). A comparison of the title pages for the Third and Fourth Folios reveals just how much visual emphasis that one word received in the later edition (fig. 4.4, 4.6). Bentley and Magnes may have been banking on this as a selling point for the volume. The title listed in their advertisement was not the *Comedies, Histories, and Tragedies*, which appeared on the title page, but rather "Shakespear's Plays."

Shakespeare's Fourth Folio offered readers a large collection of drama, but it was not the largest. That prize went to the 1679 edition of Francis Beaumont and John Fletcher's *Fifty Comedies and Tragedies*. Like Shakespeare, the playwrights Beaumont and Fletcher first had their plays published in folio before the Restoration of the Stuart monarchy in 1660. In 1647, their *Comedies and Tragedies* was published in folio with thirty-four plays and one masque. The publishers of the 1647 Beaumont and Fletcher clearly used Shakespeare's Folio as a model, especially in their use of pica roman type and double-columned pages. By 1679, a new set of publishers expanded the Beaumont and Fletcher canon by adding eighteen plays that could be attributed loosely to either author and that had been previously printed only in quarto. The notion that "more means better" was certainly marketed to customers at the time, a strategy that likely informed the decision to include the number of plays ("fifty") in the book's title. Readers who opened the 1679 Beaumont and Fletcher folio might have been surprised to find that the collection had more plays than advertised on the title page. The Catalogue enumerated fifty-one titles, and indeed, this is the number that Bentley and Magnes included in their own separately printed advertisement for the book: "*Beaumont* and *Fletchers* Plays: in all 51, in large Fol." ("Some Books printed," 1686). But even "51" was not an accurate description. Two more works not listed in the Catalogue (a masque and "Four Plays in One") were appended to the collection, bringing the total count to fifty-three dramatic works in one volume.

When the Fourth Folio was published in 1685 and Bentley and Magnes described it as a volume of forty-three plays, it was marketed and sold alongside the Beaumont and Fletcher folio. Indeed, the first "large folio" on their list was Beaumont and Fletcher's, while Shakespeare's came second. The two titles appeared together again in 1691 in a "A Catalogue of some Plays Printed for R. Bentley" (fig. 4.7). In this list, among the fifty-one plays in the Beaumont and Fletcher folio, and the forty-three in the Shakespeare Fourth Folio, is a numbered list of fifty-eight additional play titles for sale in his bookshop, plus an assortment of other collected play sets. Bentley was clearly framing his shop as the place to acquire plays, and if customers were keeping numbered tallies, more than 150 of them.

That Bentley's catalogue refers to the folio of Beaumont and Fletcher as a volume "Printed for R Bentley" is curious, because he is not identified on any copies of the 1679 folio as part of its publishing syndicate. Presumably, though, he owned some shares of the stock, and by 1685 he was ready to invest more

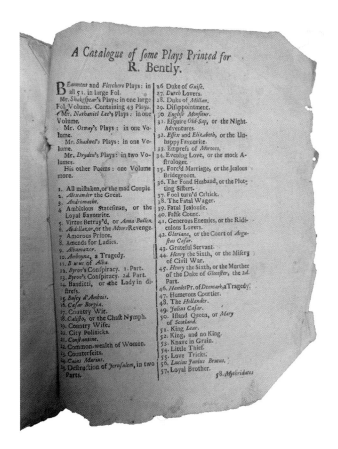

FIGURE 4.7 Bentley's Catalogue of Plays (1691). In Thomas D'Ursey's *Madam Fickle: or, The Witty False Ones* (London, 1691). The Rare Book & Manuscript Library, University of Illinois at Urbana-Champaign, IUA04322.

money in another folio of plays, the Shakespeare Fourth Folio. Another common investor in both ventures was Henry Herringman, and it is he, along with John Martyn and Richard Marriot, who announced in 1679 a new folio publication scheme. In an introductory note to the *Fifty Comedies and Tragedies* (1679), the publishers explain that the Beaumont and Fletcher folio was a marketing test: "*If our care and endeavours to do our Authors right (in an incorrupt and genuine Edition of their Works) and thereby to gratifie and oblige the Reader, be but requited with a suitable entertainment, we shall be encourag'd to bring* Ben. Johnson's *two Volumes into one, and publish them in this form; and also to reprint Old Shakespear*" (sig. A1v; italics in the original). Apparently, readers appreciated the expanded Beaumont and Fletcher folio, and the publishers stayed true to their word. Martyn and Marriot passed away before 1685, so it was Herringman's edition of "Old Shakespear" that became the Fourth Folio of 1685, collaboratively published with Bentley, Edward Brewster, and Richard Chiswell. Jonson's folio followed in 1692, published by Herringman, Chiswell, Brewster, Thomas Bassett, Matthew Wotton, and George Conyers.

What is evident in the stationers' note regarding their "care and endeavours" is that the compilation of plays in "one volume" continued to be a selling point for dramatic folios through the end of the seventeenth century. Both the Shakespeare and the Beaumont and Fletcher folios were sold as integral volumes, but as the note also indicates, Jonson's works had not. His *Works* (published in two volumes, the first in 1640 and the second in 1641) were divided into two bulky folio volumes (Connor 2014, 177). This note shows us that as early as 1679, Herringman and his syndicate were thinking about bringing "Ben Johnson's two Volumes into one." To do so, they had to put Jonson in "this form," which likely meant in large folio and with two-columns of text per page. Indeed, to fit Jonson's multi-genre works into one volume, some serious textual compression had to occur, and the two-column layout utilized in combination with the large demy sheets made it possible. Herringman and his collaborators cut the page margins to improve their profit margins.

The large folio format was also, as one might expect, an efficient way to package several texts in one volume. Demy paper was more expensive than crown, but its added height meant that more lines of text could be added to the page and thus fewer sheets of paper used overall. Demy's size was a cost-saving feature for the publishers of the Folios. Specifically, for Shakespeare's Fourth Folio, it allowed its publishers to add the seven additional plays to the collection without adding more pages to the volume. As noted above, when the Shakespeare Third Folio was reissued with the seven appended plays in 1663/64, it required approximately 257 edition sheets of crown. In 1685, when the publishers reprinted those same forty-three plays, they were able to reduce the edition to 229 sheets—just two more sheets than was required for the First Folio. That the publishers were being economical is not a surprise, but with pages packed full of dense columns of type, it does beg the question of whether the upgrade to large folio was concomitant with a downgrade in readability. That the early eighteenth century saw the works of Shakespeare, Jonson, and Beaumont and Fletcher reformatted into smaller, multivolume sets might suggest that customers had grown weary of reading plays in supersized folios.

CONCLUSION

Reducing Shakespeare's plays to countable commodities, or treating them as words that were wedged onto a crowded page, might seem to detach Shakespeare from the wonder and reverence that is frequently tethered to his literary legacy. William Prynne knew this in 1633 when he implied that readers' hunger for more plays by Shakespeare resulted not only from their sinful natures, but also from booksellers' desire for profits. Shakespeare's plays growing from quarto to folio was troubling, not just because a common playwright was garnering more attention than writers of perceived substance, but also because Prynne saw that such a trend was irreversible. Consumption might continue to be guided by which authors proved trendy and accessible, by what was bigger and advertised as better, rather than what was truly needed for oneself or the health of one's community, however defined.

Prynne would have been horrified by the fact that we continue to aggrandize Shakespeare and his Folio today. And while it's easy to dismiss his anxieties about Shakespeare as a corrupting force, Prynne's concerns do offer us some useful food for thought. As we mark the four-hundredth anniversary of the First Folio, it seems worth asking why we want "more Shakespeare," what drives our appetite for more knowledge about his authorship, more understanding of his books and their production? How can we be more cognizant of the forces, inside and outside ivory towers and museum walls, that encourage us to build him up or tear him down? What informs our decisions to serve him up in certain moments, in new forms, and in greater quantities? Celebrating the anniversary of a book that elicited varying responses in its time is an invitation to recalibrate our sense of the value that this supersized authorial figure bears in our own.

CHAPTER 5

Surviving Shakespeare
Or, What We Can Learn from 3,000 Copies
and 382 Fragments of the Plays and Poems

Zachary Lesser

No printed book has been studied so intensively as *Mr. William Shakespeares Comedies, Histories, & Tragedies* (1623), better known as the First Folio. Surviving copies of this edition have been scrutinized to help us understand its typesetting, printing, proofreading, and stop-press correction. The study of this one edition has also helped us to understand the early modern English book trade and the printing, typefounding, and paper-making industries associated with it (see Claire Bourne's chapter in this volume). The men who set the book in type have even been given pseudonyms, since we do not know their real names: "Compositor A," "Compositor B," or "Compositor E" can each be distinguished by small differences in their habitual spellings of common words. And the surviving copies of the First Folio have been catalogued in great detail, with every small tear, blotted piece of type, and missing page carefully noted (Rasmussen and West 2012). All of this attention testifies to the central place of this book in the history of English literature. But scholars have mainly been interested in understanding more about the book in its original context in 1623: In what order were the plays printed? Who put up the money for the edition and why? How many copies were printed? How much did it cost retail? They have generally been less interested in what has happened to these copies in the four centuries since 1623—in how these books have been read, bought, and sold; rebound and reconfigured; and used to record important events, or as scrap paper (fig. 5.1). And if

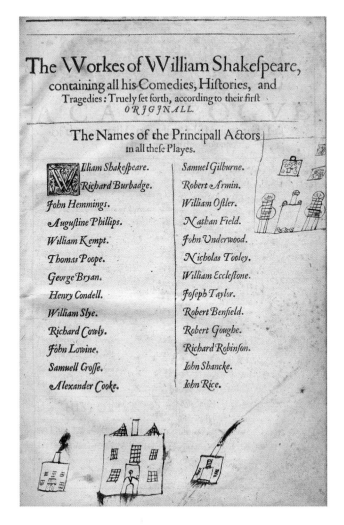

FIGURE 5.1   A copy of the First Folio at the Folger Shakespeare Library (SC 5109) includes a child's drawing of three houses and of a room with chairs, table, and wall art. These may have been by the woman who signed the other side of this page "Elizabeth Okell her Book 1729." On a blank front endpaper of the same copy someone has written: "August 4th 1914 war declared on Germany" and "Nov 11th 1918 armistice signed at 5 AM." Folger Shakespeare Library, STC 22273 Fo.1 no.78, fol. [A7r] of preliminaries.

this is true of the First Folio, it is even more true of the other three Shakespeare Folios: the Second Folio, printed in 1632; the Third Folio, printed in 1663–4; the Fourth Folio, printed in 1685; plus all the editions of Shakespeare's plays and poems printed individually in smaller formats like quarto and octavo (see Tara Lyons's chapter in this volume).

What can we learn from surviving Shakespeare? What can the long history of these books tell us about how Shakespeare has been valued, appreciated, and understood over the past four hundred years? The online *Shakespeare Census* (https://shakespearecensus.org), which I developed with Adam Hooks, attempts to locate and describe all surviving copies of all Shakespeare editions printed through 1700 (Hooks and Lesser 2022). The information it contains had previously been scattered across numerous library catalogues. Aside from the First

Folio, the other editions in the *Census* had not been included in any similar census since the early twentieth century, and some of them never at all (Bartlett and Pollard 1916; Bartlett 1939). Users of the site can browse by title, from familiar plays like *Hamlet* or *Midsummer Night's Dream*, to less-known works attributed to Shakespeare in the period but no longer considered his today, like *The Puritan* or *Sir John Oldcastle*. And they can also search by current location, previous owner's name, and specific features, such as whether a copy contains handwritten marginalia, or whether it can be associated with a previous owner from as far back as the seventeenth century. Currently the *Census* includes 3,000 more or less complete copies and 382 fragments (copies including fewer than half their original pages) of the forty titles it surveys. By gathering all of this information about these copies in one place, the *Shakespeare Census* offers us new perspectives on the history of Shakespeare and his work, both at the large scale of datasets and at the small scale of individual owners, their copies, and the stories they tell.

This book, and its accompanying exhibition at the Frick Art Museum in Pittsburgh and Carnegie Mellon University Libraries, just like similar exhibitions around the world in 2023, are all due to the First Folio. It is the most famous and treasured Shakespeare edition. One particularly well-preserved copy recently sold at auction for nearly $10 million, to a rare book dealer who no doubt believes (or already knows) he can sell it on to a private collector for substantially more than that. This copy was sold by Mills College to raise funds to avert a budget crisis that threatened the existence of the school. (Despite the sale, the school closed in 2022, merging with Northeastern University.) In the *Shakespeare Census*, which assigns a unique reference number to every surviving copy and fragment, this is the copy identified as SC 5173. Over the years, like many copies of the First Folio, it has been repeatedly auctioned and sold, passing through the hands of at least five dealers and auction houses, its price increasing along the way.

Contrary to what is often assumed, the financial value of the First Folio has very little to do with its rarity. The *Shakespeare Census* records 228 copies of the First Folio, which is certainly fewer than the 373 copies of the Second Folio, or the 339 copies of the Fourth Folio. (Since books printed in the later seventeenth century tend to survive in significantly higher numbers today than those printed in the earlier part of the century, I suspect that the Fourth will ultimately surpass the Second because many copies in private hands are currently unaccounted for in the *Census*.) But the rarest of the Folios, by far, is the Third, with only 182 copies surviving today. Why is the Third so much harder to find today than the others? This edition was published in 1663, and then quickly revised in 1664 when a new title page was printed that highlighted seven additional plays—the so-called Shakespeare Apocrypha—that were added on at the end. Two years later, the Great Fire destroyed most of the buildings in London, including the old wooden St. Paul's Cathedral, where many booksellers' shops were located. It seems likely that many unsold sheets of the Third Folio went up in flames, creating a relative scarcity that persists today. If books were valued simply by their rarity, the Third Folio would sell for much higher prices than the First.

None of the Folios however (not even the Third) can approach the rarity of Shakespeare's plays and poems that were printed individually. Here are the top twenty Shakespeare editions, excluding apocryphal titles, according to the number of their surviving copies at the time of writing:

Year	Title	Surviving copies
1632	Second Folio	373
1685	Fourth Folio	339
1623	First Folio	228
1663	Third Folio	182
1640	Poems	66
1634	*Two Noble Kinsmen*	59
1619	*Henry V*	45
1619	*The Whole Contention (2 & 3 Henry VI)*	42
1691	*Julius Caesar*	39
1619	*King Lear*	38
1619	*Merry Wives of Windsor*	38
1684	*Julius Caesar*	38
1695	*Othello*	37
1619	*Pericles*	36
1619	*Midsummer Night's Dream*	34
1637	*Hamlet*	34
1630	*Othello*	33
1619	*Merchant of Venice*	33
1687	*Othello*	32
1637	*Romeo and Juliet*	31

The first thing to notice about this list is the massive drop-off after the Folios. Even the most common Shakespeare quarto survives in only a third of the number of copies of the rarest Folio. (In 2022, a copy of the 1640 *Poems* [SC 1114.7] sold at auction for $37,500, well above the auction house's estimate, but a tiny fraction of the price of a First Folio.) The second thing to notice is that none of these editions was printed during Shakespeare's lifetime, since, as noted above,

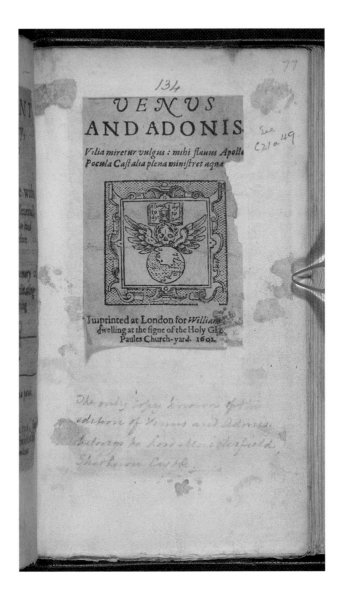

FIGURE 5.2 The only surviving evidence for the tenth edition of *Venus and Adonis*, pasted into a scrapbook by John Bagford. © British Library Board, Harl. 5990 (134).

books printed later in the seventeenth century tend to survive in greater numbers. For all Shakespeare editions printed through 1616, only 6.3 copies survive on average. Fourteen editions of Shakespeare titles survive in only a single copy, including the first editions of *Titus Andronicus* (SC 1523), *Venus and Adonis* (SC 1648), and *Henry VI Part 3* (SC 362). The first edition of *Hamlet* survives in only two copies (SC 28 and 29), neither of which was known to exist prior to the 1820s. The first edition of *Henry IV Part 1* survives only in a fragment of eight pages (SC 191). Of an edition of *Venus and Adonis* probably printed around 1610, only the title page survives, pasted into a scrapbook of other printed fragments by the seventeenth-century magpie John Bagford (SC 1664) (Trettien 2021, 183–258) (fig. 5.2). This poem was immensely popular: we know of seventeen editions between 1593 and 1675. Overall, we can estimate that something like twenty to thirty thousand copies of *Venus and Adonis* were printed before 1700, but today only twenty-four survive, along with four fragments.

We could have lost many of these editions entirely, and we can be fairly certain we have lost a few others, including some of *Venus and Adonis* (see Farmer 2016). A play called *Love's Labors Won* was mentioned in a list of Shakespeare's plays in 1598 by a contemporary commentator on English poetry. For a long time, it was assumed this was an error, or perhaps an alternative title for another Shakespeare play. In 1953, however, a scrap of paper used to stabilize the binding of another book was discovered to be a page of a provincial bookseller's inventory (or perhaps a customer's order of books from that bookseller), and this list includes an entry for *Love's Labors Won* (Baldwin 1957). We can assume that a play with this title was indeed printed, therefore, but not a page of it survives.

What accounts for the hugely increased chances of survival of the four Folios compared to the individual editions, even those printed later? The answer is simple: size. The bigger the book, the more durable it was, and the greater the number of copies that survive to this day. Furthermore, big books were generally bound, encased between hard boards that again increased their chances of survival. Short items like single plays were sold "stab-stitched," a much less durable method of holding the printed sheets together by punching them with an awl two or three times along the inner margin and running string through them (Pratt 2015). Notice that among the individual plays and poems on the list above, nearly half were published in 1619, and the reason is similar: this group of plays was printed to be sold bound all together as part of the first attempt, four years before the First Folio, to market a collection of Shakespeare's plays. The 1619 quartos survive now almost always as single items—because they were disbound and rebound as precious treasures in the eighteenth and nineteenth centuries—but their higher rate of survival indicates that they were originally purchased as part of a large, bound book (Lesser 2021).

When we look at the broader context of surviving Shakespeare, then, it turns out that the First Folio, like the other Folios, is not rare at all. It is a common book. In a way, though, the higher survival of the Folios has contributed to their value, because there are many more copies that remain available for purchase through auctions and dealers compared with the quartos. Only seventy-one copies of Shakespeare's individual plays and poems in the *Census* are currently in private hands, a little under 4 percent of the total; the other copies are in institutional libraries, highly unlikely ever to appear on the market. In reality, there are certainly more copies than this in private collections, especially of the later seventeenth-century quartos, because these are harder to locate and hence less likely to appear in the *Census* than institutional copies. Nonetheless, the contrast with the Folios is clear: of the 1122 folios in the *Census*, 168 copies (14.9 percent) are still in private hands. About one in eleven surviving copies of the First Folio (twenty of 228) is still owned privately, and these have been sold again and again over the years, so that every few years, a copy appears for sale at auction. Shakespeare's overwhelming cultural importance, combined with the relative availability of the First Folio compared to the individually printed plays, has created a highly desirable luxury commodity for billionaires around the world.

This has long been the case: where money goes, Shakespeare and his First Folio follow. Well over half of the surviving copies of the First Folio are now in the United States, mainly acquired in the late-nineteenth-century Gilded Age. The immense wealth of a small number of American collectors, combined with the decay of English landed estates, especially following the institution of the modern estate tax in the UK in 1894, resulted in a huge migration of Shakespeare across the Atlantic. Henry Folger purchased more than anyone else, eighty-two copies of the First Folio alone, and his library now holds 652 items listed in the *Census* (including fragments), more than three times the next institution, Oxford University (185 items). Folger made his fortune in oil, serving as president of John D. Rockefeller's Standard Oil. His fellow collectors, auction rivals, and Gilded Age tycoons Henry Huntington and J. P. Morgan dominated the California railroad and New York finance industries. The libraries they founded now hold 164 and thirty-one items in the *Census*, respectively.

The first major collector of Shakespeare in the United States was Thomas Pennant Barton, who had begun collecting about half a century earlier than Folger, Huntington, and Morgan. Barton's collection, now at the Boston Public Library, included a First Folio, two Second Folios, two Third Folios (one in the very rare 1663 state), a Fourth Folio, and sixty-one individual plays and poems. Barton's money mainly came through marriage to Cora Livingston, heir to an old New York family that included signers of the Declaration of Independence and the Constitution. Numerous other American institutions own copies of Shakespeare acquired in these years by the mega-rich of their time, including the Astors (New York Public Library), the Wideners (Harvard University, Free Library of Philadelphia), James Lenox (New York Public Library), the mining engineer and San Francisco mayor Alfred Sutro (California State Library, Sutro), the president of the New York Stock Exchange Brayton Ives (Princeton University), the railroad magnate Henry Walters (Walters Art Museum), and the pioneering car manufacturer Charles Clifton (Buffalo and Erie County Public Library).

Where money goes, there goes Shakespeare: the trend continued in the late twentieth century as numerous copies moved to Japan. After the Folger, with its eighty-two copies of the First Folio, the largest collection is now at Meisei University just outside Tokyo. Meisei holds 114 items currently listed in the *Census*, making it the seventh largest collection worldwide, with eleven First Folios, twenty-six Second Folios, twenty-three Third Folios, and twenty-six Fourth Folios, along with numerous individually printed plays and poems. Other large holdings of Shakespeare outside the anglophone world include the Martin Bodmer Foundation in Geneva, which has forty-two copies, including one of each Folio and first editions of *Much Ado About Nothing*, *Henry IV Part 2*, the *Sonnets*, *Troilus and Cressida*, and *Othello*, and the Bibliothèque National de France (BnF), which has eighteen copies in the *Census*, including all four Folios. The Bodmer collection was put together in the mid-twentieth century, and the BnF mainly acquired its Shakespeare in the mid-nineteenth century. The University and City Library of Cologne also has a full set of the Folios, purchased along with a copy of the *Poems* in 1960, and the State Library of Württemberg acquired their four Folios around the same year. The First Folio in the Berlin State Library was given by King William I of Prussia in 1859, and the library also has a copy of the Third and Fourth Folios. In these collections we can see the global reach of Shakespeare and his books. By the nineteenth century, holding a copy of the First Folio, and a set of all four folios, had become an aspirational mark of distinction for any institution.

Other libraries in the non-anglophone world have copies of Shakespeare that testify not to his later canonization as the pinnacle of English literature, but rather to the more mundane journeys made by people and books in the Renaissance. The Zurich Central Library has quartos of the 1609 *Romeo and Juliet* (SC 1368), the 1611 *Hamlet* (SC 55), and the 1611 *Pericles* (SC 1006.5) that were brought back to Switzerland by travelers to London in 1613 and have remained there ever since (Erne 2023). The University of Wroclaw in Poland holds a 1611 *Hamlet* (SC 36) that is bound up with five other English texts and two in Dutch, almost certainly gathered together by an early seventeenth-century traveler. The State Library of Hamburg has a similar composite volume of thirteen items, including a 1609 *Pericles* (SC 1002), with the label "Anglicana Varia"—various works in English—on the back cover. Clearly foreign visitors were buying Shakespeare along with other souvenirs in the bookshops of London. Some of these copies have turned up only recently in libraries where they had not been previously noticed, and it is entirely possible that there remain copies of Shakespeare still to be found in continental European libraries.

Shakespeare also made his way to the Continent in folio in the seventeenth century. A First Folio at the University of Padua, which is heavily marked up for performances of *Measure for Measure*, *Winter's Tale*, and *Macbeth*, seems by

FIGURE 5.3 The First Folio now at the University of Padova was heavily marked up for performance. This page of *Macbeth* adds cues for offstage sounds ("Knock") and prepares actors for their coming entrances ("Lady," "Macduff / Lenox," and so on). The Porter's famous speech was marked for cutting in performance. University of Padova and Internet Culturale, RARI.N.S.1, p. 137.

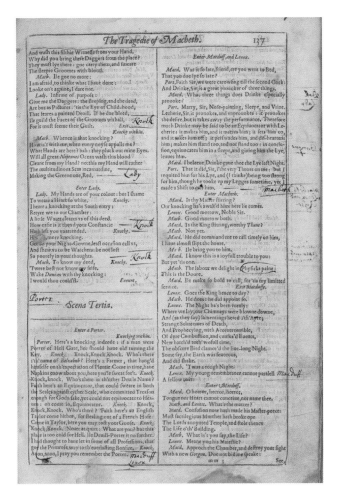

the 1640s to have been in the house of the leader of the English merchants in Venice, and then in the library of English students studying in Padua (fig. 5.3, SC 5003; also see Prosdocimi 2021). A copy of the Second Folio traveled with English Catholics to the seminary in Valladolid, Spain, where it was censored to remove blasphemy and obscenity, perhaps for school performance (fig. 5.4, SC 6202). And in 2014, a First Folio was discovered by the librarian in the collection of Saint-Omer, France, having long been mistaken for an eighteenth-century edition since it is missing its title page (SC 5004). Like the Valladolid Second Folio, this First Folio was connected with English Catholics, probably given to the Jesuit College in Saint-Omer in the seventeenth or early eighteenth century, and it too is marked up for student performance (Mayer 2015).

It is remarkable that "new" copies of the First Folio still turn up. Another copy hiding in plain sight was found in 2016 in the library at Mount Stuart on the Isle of Bute, Scotland (SC 5151). This copy, once owned by the eighteenth-century

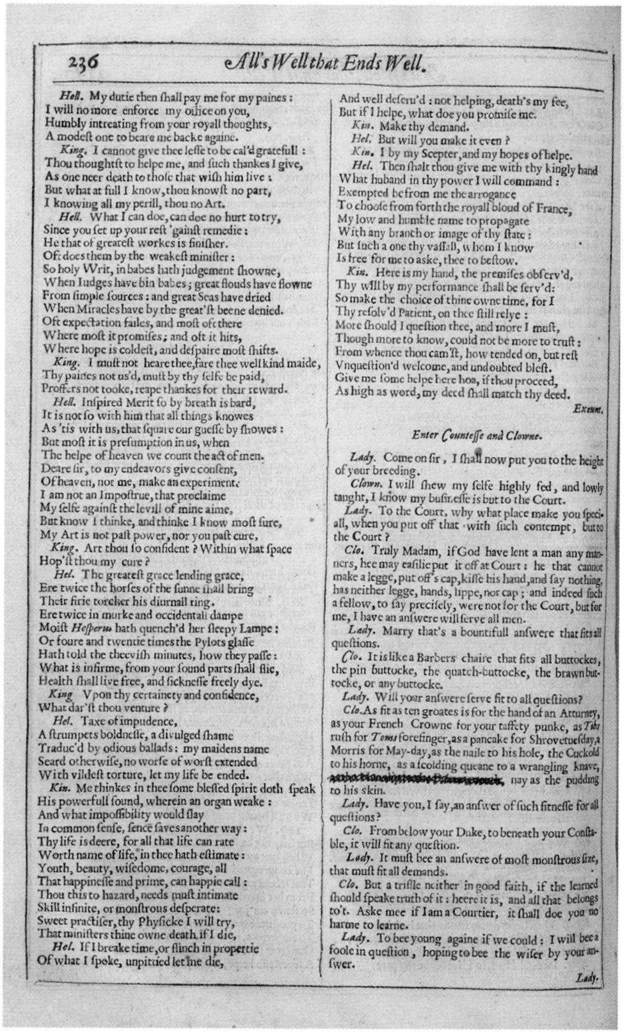

FIGURE 5.4   A page from *All's Well That Ends Well* in a Second Folio that was censored at the English seminary in Valladolid, Spain. Here the censor tried to make illegible the Clown's assertion that he has an answer as suitable for all questions "as the Nuns lip to the Friers mouth," a typical bit of English anti-Catholic satire. Folger Shakespeare Library, STC 22274 Fo.2 no.07, p. 236.

Shakespearean editor Isaac Reed, is divided into three volumes, one for each genre in the collection (Smith 2016b). Like the Saint-Omer copy, this First Folio had been there for well over a century, but had simply been forgotten. If this seems hard to believe, we should remember that the First Folio has not always been as highly valued as it is today. For the merchants who took it to Venice, or the students in Padua or Saint-Omer, it was no doubt a useful book, bringing together many plays in a single volume that could be easily transported, but it was not a cherished treasure.

There is no better example of these shifting ideas about the value of the First Folio than the case of the Bodleian Library copy (SC 5161). The Bodleian was founded in 1602 and in 1610 it became England's first deposit library, supposed to receive one copy of every book published. While not all publishers actually followed this regulation, the publishers of the First Folio did, and the Bodleian accounts record that a First Folio was sent to the library's binder on February 17, 1624 (see Lyons 2023). In 1664, the Third Folio appeared with its seven additional plays—only one of which, *Pericles*, is now widely considered to be (in part) by Shakespeare. But to the librarians at the Bodleian, their copy of the Third Folio looked "new and improved," and so they deaccessioned their old, seemingly incomplete First Folio. Centuries later, in 1905, an Oxford undergraduate brought his family's copy of the First Folio to the librarian at the Bodleian for inspection. The librarian recognized it as the very one that had been sold off in the 1660s, still in its original binding. But the Bodleian could not afford to match the huge offer made by an unknown American millionaire (Henry Folger)—until a national campaign appealing to British patriotism managed to raise the funds, and the book returned to the Bodleian after two and a half centuries (Smith 2016a).

This story gets at a key underlying transformation in the history of editing Shakespeare, and thus in the history of our conceptions of authorship more broadly. The Bodleian's decision to deaccession their First Folio makes good sense in the context of seventeenth-century ideas about texts. Successive editions of a work could be improved, or in the contemporary word, "perfected," through corrections not only of typographical and other printing errors but also of misunderstood words, grammatical confusions, or other linguistic infelicities. It made little difference who was making these changes, whether it was the author, a reader, reviser, a proofreader in the printshop, or simply the compositor setting the type. Texts, it was believed, were made more perfect over time through an iterative process of improvement (Massai 2007, 3–11). Hence when Nicholas Rowe began working on his 1709 edition of Shakespeare's works (the first "complete works" edition after the four Folios), he naturally started working from a copy of the Fourth Folio, the most recent and most "perfected." It was only later in the eighteenth-century that a complete reversal in editorial theory mandated returning to the *earliest* editions, those closest to the author's hand, and thus began to relegate the Second, Third, and Fourth Folios, as well as later editions of the plays in quarto, to "non-authoritative" status. No editor of Shakespeare today would begin with the text of one of the later Folios, because we now see successive reprinting—without any authorial input—as irrelevant and simply liable to introduce new textual error. Only after this shift in our understanding of authorship could the First Folio become the most highly prized of Shakespeare's books, because it could now be imagined to offer privileged access to Shakespeare's mind.

The Bodleian copy of the First Folio thus reveals something important simply through its provenance, or its history of ownership. Other copies of the First Folio can tell us new stories about Shakespeare because of the unique marks left in them by past readers. The copy at the Free Library of Philadelphia (SC 5114), for instance, is heavily annotated, and recently two scholars, Claire Bourne and Jason Scott-Warren, have made the persuasive argument that the annotations are by the English poet and author of the biblical epic *Paradise Lost*, John Milton (Bourne and Scott-Warren 2022). Here we have a famous author reading a famous author, and the marginalia promise to illuminate the influence of one of England's greatest poets on another. But an annotated copy at Meisei University seems just as fascinating and important to me, and in this case the annotator is not famous; indeed we cannot even be sure who it was, although it may have been the William Johnstoune who wrote his name on one of its pages (SC 5139). This copy shows an early reader responding in detail to Shakespeare's plays, sometimes in ways that are strikingly different than we might expect. For example, most modern productions of *Hamlet* make Polonius into an old fool, constantly dispensing bits of supposed wisdom that turn out to be tired clichés. The actors playing Laertes and Ophelia often make faces behind his back as he gives them his trite advice: "Neither a borrower nor a lender be"; "To thine own self be true." For the Meisei reader, however, Polonius's speeches in this scene are full of practical advice that can be extracted from the play and used on similar occasions. Hence this reader noted on this page of the folio: "Wise precepts of a father to a sonne going to trauell In foraine countries"; and "a fathers wise counsell to his doghter not to beleeue the promises and oathes of a young professed louer" (fig. 5.5). This sort of reading that searches for interesting snippets to copy, known as commonplacing, was practiced far more often in Shakespeare's day than our own, although many people still keep notebooks in which they record favorite lines from their books (see Estill 2015; Meyer 2018, 137–73; August 2022, 126–76). At another point, when Hamlet is mocking Polonius for having a "plentiful lack of wit," the annotator, again preparing to extract these lines into a commonplace book, glossed them as "defects of old men." Polonius can seem wise or foolish to this reader, with no apparent contradiction, because these different moments do not need to cohere into a single, unified character. To the commonplacing reader of this First Folio, the plot, characters, and themes of the play are less important than the proverbial wisdom it contains, which can then be recycled as the reader's own (see Lesser 2015, 200–5).

In discussing this copy, as you may have noticed, I have carefully avoided gendering the annotator with a pronoun. When we cannot be sure who wrote a bit of marginalia, we should not assume it was a man, despite the fact that in

FIGURE 5.5 A reader of this First Folio at Meisei University in Japan made extensive notes while gathering "commonplaces" for later contemplation or reuse. Meisei University, MR 774, p. 156.

early modern England, men were more likely than women to be able to read and write. Numerous copies of Shakespeare books testify that early modern women claimed them as their own. However, many of their inscriptions have been hiding in plain sight; scholars had paid little attention to them until feminist book historians began to stress their importance. The extent to which early modern women valued these books is suggested by one of Carnegie Mellon University's copies of the Fourth Folio. This copy is inscribed by Alice Brownlowe (1659–1721) and by her daughters, Alice and Margaret, indicating a matrilineal reception of Shakespeare at Belton House, the Brownlowes' Lincolnshire home (fig. 5.6). Other readers did more than sign their names. A copy of the 1655 edition of *Othello* now at the University of Pennsylvania was once owned by the seventeenth-century collector Frances Wolfreston (SC 897), who wrote her usual ownership inscription on the first page of the play: "frances wolfreston her bouk." After reading the play, she returned to the same page to write her judgment of it in a different ink: "a sad one"—a pointed if terse bit of literary criticism on *Othello* (fig. 5.7). Wolfreston had one of the most extensive collections of play quartos in the seventeenth century, and her library is currently being reconstructed virtually by Sarah Lindenbaum. Thirteen copies in the *Shakespeare Census* are known to have once been owned by Wolfreston. Her brief literary remarks also appear on a copy of *Taming of the Shrew* (1631) now at the Boston Public Library: "a very prity mery one of a [. . .] begar found by a lord who persuaded him he was a lord, and this play was playd befor his new lordship" (SC 1475); on a copy of *Merchant of Venice* (1637) also at the Boston Public Library ("the rich jue would have a £ of flesh of his creditor" [SC 670]) and on a copy of *King Lear* (1655) at the British Library ("a prity one" [SC 522]). Wolfreston also owned the unique surviving copy of the 1593 first edition of *Venus and Adonis* (SC 1648). This tale seems to be one that she particularly enjoyed, since she also owned a copy of the 1636 edition of *Venus and Adonis* (SC 1672), as well as a copy of the poetic anthology *Englands Helicon*, in which she singled out Henry Constable's poem, "The Shepherd's Song of Venus and Adonis." Until their auction in 1856, Wolfreston's books had remained in more or less their original condition at the Wolfreston family house "in a corner of the library time out of mind, unnoticed and unheeded" (Lindenbaum 2018).

Another example of early book ownership by a seventeenth-century woman can be found on a copy of the second quarto of *Romeo and Juliet* at Yale University (SC 1361). Owned by Elisabeth Rotton, it contains an anagram on her name, a common early modern parlor game: "Her lot is to b neat." Did she write this herself, or did someone else? Is it meant as praise, suggesting that she is "neat" in the sense that Ben Jonson praises Lady Sidney in "To Penshurst"? There Jonson writes that, when King James unexpectedly turned up, Lady Sidney "reaped / The just reward of her high housewifery; / To have her linen, plate, and all things nigh, / When she was far; and not a room but dressed / As if it had expected such a guest!" Or is this a complaint written by Rotton? Her "lot," a kind of drudgery, is to be neat, to tend to housewifery, when she might want to be doing something else.* Like a lot of marginalia in early Shakespeare books, this anagram offers tantalizing evidence of a broader social world of reading, but can also leave us frustrated at our inability to fully reconstruct that world.

In the case of numerous other copies, all we have is a name: "Elizabeth Copinger" on a copy of *Henry IV Part 1* at Trinity College, Cambridge (SC 205); "Mary Shipp" on a First Folio at Colgate University (SC 5023); "Mary Child is

---

*I am thankful to Tiffany Stern for sharing her unpublished work on Rotton.

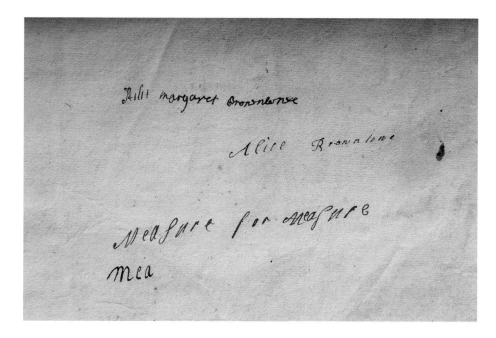

FIGURE 5.6   The signatures of Alice Brownlowe (1659–1721) and her daughters, Alice (?) and Margaret, evidently in imitation of their mother's hand. Carnegie Mellon University Libraries, Special Collections, Posner PR2751 .A4 1685.

FIGURE 5.7   Frances Wolfreston's ownership mark and comment on her copy of the 1655 *Othello*. Kislak Center for Special Collections, Rare Books, and Manuscripts, University of Pennsylvania, Furness Collection, EC Sh155.622oc, p. 1.

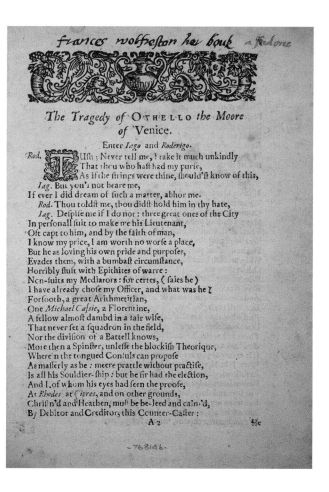

the true possessor of this booke" on a First Folio at the Folger (SC 5054); "Dorothy P." on a copy of *Two Noble Kinsmen* at the University of Glasgow (SC 1620); "Elizabeth Bourne her boock" (crossed out) and "Dorothy Cowper" and "Martha King," all on *The Rape of Lucrece* at the Bodmer Foundation, Geneva (SC 1192). And many others. We cannot always discover much more about who these women were, but their presence in these books testifies to the fact that from the beginning, women were buying and reading Shakespeare and marking these books as theirs.

More unusual is the occasional glimpse of working-class readers. A volume at Petworth House, the aristocratic home of the earls of Northumberland, gathers ten plays together, including a copy of the 1619 edition of *Henry V* (SC 337). On the last page of Robert Greene's *A Looking-Glass for London and England* (1617) is the inscription: "y[ou]r Louinge ffreind ffase the hows Coopper." Fase was likely the "house cooper" (or barrel-maker) at Petworth, and his marginalia may well be the earliest example of someone who identified as a craftsperson writing in a Renaissance English playbook. In another volume at Petworth, someone wrote a little rhyme on the blank final page of a 1613 *Thomas Lord Cromwell* (SC 1515), one of the Shakespeare apocrypha: "Niccolas ffass the [. . .] is base." Part of the inscription has been trimmed during a later rebinding, but a good guess is that the missing word is "cooper." Who is writing this insult, a fellow servant at Petworth? Was it meant playfully or viciously? Fase's inscription—practicing a formal close to a letter, "your loving friend"—suggests that he was interested in acquiring learning and decorous manners. Perhaps this other writer is mocking Fase's perceived striving for advancement? Whatever story lies behind the two inscriptions, here we have evidence of servants taking the liberty not only of leafing through books in the Petworth library, but also of writing in them.

We are fortunate that these marks of previous reading and ownership survive, because by the nineteenth century, as Shakespeare's books became ever more precious, they were frequently washed, bleached, and otherwise cleaned by booksellers and collectors in an attempt to make them "pristine" and "perfect." Removed from their earlier bindings, and often from composite volumes like the ones at Petworth that held six or eight or ten plays together, the sheets of a play were easily accessible for cleaning and other kinds of manipulation before they were put into bespoke bindings for these new collectors. The actor John Philip Kemble (1757–1823) trimmed the margins of each leaf of his three to four thousand plays and inlaid them into new paper before rebinding them. In this way, he could eliminate manuscript marginalia, standardize the size of his plays before he put them into his own composite volumes, and remove tears and other damage to the pages. Kemble's collection was acquired by the Duke of Devonshire, and the Devonshire collection was acquired by Henry Huntington in 1914, by which time it included about 7,500 plays, among them numerous Shakespeare copies. Huntington had them rebound again, typically putting his most highly prized copies, including Shakespeare, in individual luxury bindings. Even aside from Kemble's radical trimming of the pages of his plays, each rebinding of a book generally requires some trimming of the margins. For this reason, books that have been rebound multiple times over the years, like many Shakespeare copies, have typically been heavily trimmed. Quite a lot of early signs of readings in the margins of these plays is surely lost to us today (Pratt 2019).

Once they were removed from earlier bindings, plays could also be "sophisticated," with the best pages from different copies combined to form a single complete one. For nineteenth-century collectors, the best pages typically were clean pages, without marginalia or other signs of previous use. It is almost impossible today to determine how many First Folios have been sophisticated in this way. As the most desirable Shakespeare books, they have certainly been subjected to more manipulation than others. No page was more necessary for a collector than the title page with its engraved portrait, and many copies of the First Folio today have the portrait or the entire title page supplied from a different copy, or even from a copy of a later Folio. The Marquess of Northampton's copy (SC 5135), for instance, reproduces the lettering on its title page in facsimile, but the portrait itself, like the other preliminary pages, comes from a copy of the Second Folio (Rasmussen and West 2012, 164). And a copy once owned by an early eighteenth-century woman named Elizabeth Okell (SC 5109) also includes the title page from the Second Folio, but where the wording obviously differs from the First, as in the imprint, the text has been cut out and patched with a printed facsimile (fig. 5.8).

In the same way, the major Victorian collector and scholar James Orchard Halliwell-Phillipps (1820–99) sometimes used multiple copies of the same edition to make a better one, giving away the now less-perfect copy to a friend or fellow collector. He gave one copy of *The Taming of the Shrew* (1631) to Horace Howard Furness (1833–1912), for example. The Furness copy (SC 1497) lacks the date in the imprint, because it was cut out and neatly replaced with a blank patch by Halliwell-Phillipps's preferred binder, Francis Bedford. That bit of paper with the date was then inserted into the copy that Halliwell-Phillipps kept for himself (SC 1482), which was better in other respects but damaged around the imprint date (Lesser 2021, 184n57). He also cut up copies of Shakespeare Folios and quartos and pasted the fragments into scrapbooks, often as part of his own work toward an edition of the complete works—a way of appreciating Shakespeare's books that is strikingly alien to our own sensibilities (Salzman 2021).

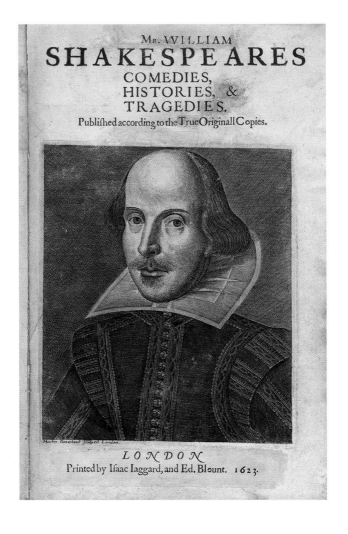

FIGURE 5.8 A composite created by patching a Second Folio title page with newly printed sections designed to replace sections that were damaged or that differed too greatly from the typography of the First Folio. Folger Shakespeare Library, STC 22273 Fo.1 no.78.

London booksellers like Thomas Rodd, who was Thomas Barton's main contact in the trade, had a wide variety of similar techniques at their disposal for making books more attractive to their clients. Rodd sold Barton several Shakespeare plays with previously torn title pages: "The copies of the *Yorkshire Tragedy* & the *Merry Wives* have titles repaired, the date of each being filled in by fac simile. This is however so admirably done that it would be impossible even for a practiced eye to detect it: still it would be dishonourable to neglect making it known to you" (Lesser 2021, 92). These copies (SC 1722, SC 716) were repaired so skillfully that they are hard to detect even today: the paper has been patched seamlessly with pages kept for this purpose in a "hospital" of damaged early printed books, and the missing date has been handwritten in pen facsimile in a near-perfect imitation of letterpress printing. The title page of Carnegie Mellon University's copy of the First Folio was likewise repaired and filled in by pen facsimile lettering that is subtle enough to be nearly undetectable.

Highly talented artists like John Harris could produce an entire title page in facsimile to supply a defective copy, as he did for the copy now at Dartmouth College (fig. 5.9, SC 5028). Harris was so renowned that he displayed his work at the Great Exhibition at Crystal Palace in 1851, and his work for the British Museum was "so perfectly done," according to a contemporary account, that the librarian Anthony Panizzi ordered "that in future all additions made to a book in facsimile should be marked as being so in a note at the bottom of the page," so that the librarians themselves would not become confused (Lesser 2021, 93). Harris's tiny signature appears on numerous title pages in the British Library today, and his work can be found on copies of the Shakespeare First and Second Folios, as well as numerous individual plays and poems.

FIGURE 5.9 A hand-drawn facsimile title page, done with pen, ink, and tracing paper by the Victorian master of the craft, John Harris. The other preliminary pages are likewise in facsimile, as are the last three leaves of the Folio; the opening and closing pages of books were the most likely to be damaged. Harris signed his name on two of the facsimile pages in this copy at Dartmouth College, Hickmott 1. Courtesy of Dartmouth Library.

These techniques for making a book "perfect" were generally not meant to deceive, but they obviously lent themselves to more underhanded activity as well. The English dealer Thomas James Wise often created playbooks from pages originating in different copies, some of them too damaged to sell in their original form. As Aaron Pratt has shown, Wise kept the best copy for himself, then sold the next best to the American collector John Wrenn (1841–1911), whose books are now at the Harry Ransom Center at the University of Texas. Sometimes Wise had a third or even a fourth copy, which he would sell to other, less wealthy collectors like the British civil servant George Aitken (1860–1917). Like Thomas Rodd, Wise generally alerted his clients to the work he had done to make their books perfect, writing to Wrenn in 1904 about a copy of John Dryden's *Marriage à la Mode*: "I found a very imperfect copy in a bundle of imperfect plays which I have, and fortunately it had the two leaves which in your copy had been supplied from a copy of the Third Edition. So now the book is all right!" (Pratt 2019, 38). But Wise went beyond simply sophisticating copies with the standard techniques of nineteenth-century bibliophiles. In 1956, the scholar David Foxon discovered through minute bibliographical examination that Wise had sliced pages out of plays at the British Museum (which had until then been thought simply to be imperfect) and then incorporated them into his own copies to make up deficiencies (Foxon 1956). Faced with all the ways that earlier bookdealers, binders, and collectors could manipulate their Shakespeare, it can be difficult to know exactly what we are seeing when we examine a particular copy.

Behind all of these increasingly expert techniques for repairing damage, supplying gaps, cleaning pages of previous owners' marks, disbinding and rebinding—behind all of this expertise, of course, was money, the money to be made from Shakespeare. As they became luxury objects in the eighteenth and nineteenth centuries, Shakespeare's books inevitably became enmeshed in the oppression and exploitation that generated so much of the immense wealth of many of these book collectors. Remember the first great American collector, Thomas Barton, whose collection was enabled by the wealth of his wife Cora Livingston? Cora's mother Louise d'Avezac fled Haiti in 1791 as the revolution began; her family were large sugarcane planters and enslaved nearly a thousand people. After arriving in New Orleans, she met Cora's father Robert Livingston, bringing much wealth to the marriage according to the *Albany Centinel*, which described her as "majestic in person and elegant in her manners, with a *long* purse!" (*Albany Centinel* 1805, emphasis in the original). The Livingston family's investment in the slave trade goes back further than that, however: one of the patriarchs of the family, Philip Livingston (1716–78), made a fortune by speculating financially on enslaved people. Barton's Shakespeare collection was financed in part by this family wealth.

Other copies have even more direct connections to slavery: the record-breaking Mills College copy auctioned for nearly $10 million in 2020 was owned in the eighteenth century by "Mad Jack" Fuller, who enslaved over 250 people on his two sugar plantations in Jamaica and argued forcefully in favor of slavery while serving as a member of Parliament. A First Folio (SC 5157) that joined the New York Public Library collection when it integrated the Astor Library had once been owned by Richard Grenville, First Duke of Buckingham and Chandos, who also enslaved people in Jamaica and made several claims for compensation when Parliament abolished slavery in the British Caribbean in 1833. (This same aristocratic family also owned a portrait that may well be of Shakespeare, known today as the "Chandos portrait.") And the Astor Library itself was created with a fortune made in part through the trade in cotton produced under slavery. One of the earliest known owners of the First Folio now at the Elizabethan Club at Yale University was George Hibbert, a leading proslavery figure who served as Chairman of the Society of West India Merchants. His wealth derived from numerous Jamaican plantations, or their lucrative mortgages, which enslaved thousands of people, and his family received over £100,000 in compensation upon abolition.

Numerous other Folios were owned by prominent figures in the East India Company, such as Dudley Coutts Marjoribanks, director of the Company in 1853, whose First Folio is now at the Folger Shakespeare Library (SC 5050) and whose Second Folio is among the books given by the automotive magnate Charles Clifton to the Buffalo and Erie County Public Library (SC 6165). The copy displayed to millions of visitors in the foyer of the reconstructed Shakespeare's Globe in London (SC 5176), on loan from a private collector, was once owned by Thomas Munro, governor of Madras for the Company from 1819 until his death in 1827. Richard Warner was a director of the Company in 1860; he later donated his collection of the four Folios, along with three individual plays, to Wadham College, Oxford.

Like many institutions, Wadham College has recently been grappling with its history as a "direct or indirect beneficiary of colonialism and Atlantic slavery." These efforts have focused on a commemorative window in the College's chapel that honors William Burge, a pro-slavery campaigner and attorney general of Jamaica before abolition. The College has commissioned a replacement panel by a Black artist from Mississippi who "has proposed incorporating in a repurposed form pieces of the old glass" (Oxford and Colonialism, n.d.). Similarly, at Yale University, where George Hibbert's copy of the First Folio now resides, John Calhoun's name was removed from one of the colleges in 2017, and stained-glass windows featuring racist imagery were replaced after a worker in the dining hall forced the issue by smashing one. Museums have also struggled to account for the histories of exploitation and extraction embodied in their art collections.

There has been less public discussion of these issues in rare book libraries, but these collections too are suffused with the same legacies, given the links between eighteenth- and nineteenth-century wealth, the slave trade, and colonialism. My examples above were not exactly chosen at random, but with an hour of time spent on the *Shakespeare Census* and the Centre for the Study of the Legacies of British Slavery, one could easily add many more copies to this list. Writing of "cultural treasures," Walter Benjamin famously claimed: "There is no document of civilization which is not at the same time a document of barbarism." His following sentence is less well-known but perhaps even more important to remember during this year of First Folio celebrations and exhibitions: "And just as such a document is not free of barbarism, barbarism taints also the manner in which it was transmitted from one owner to another." Shakespeare's books are no exception. The greatest works of literature and art, Benjamin continued, "owe their existence not only to the efforts of the great minds and talents who have created them"—and Shakespeare was certainly that—"but also to the anonymous toil of their contemporaries" (Benjamin 1968, 256). And also, we might add, to the anonymous toil of all those who—some knowingly and willingly, others very much not so—enabled the surviving copies of Shakespeare's books to be passed down to us today in the multitudinous forms that we encounter them. Shakespeare himself is commemorated and celebrated on anniversaries like this one, but how might surviving Shakespeare help us to remember *them*?

CHAPTER 6

 Everything There Is to Be Learned About Seventeenth-Century Types

Computational Bibliography and the Fourth Folio's Printers

Samuel V. Lemley, Nikolai Vogler, Christopher N. Warren, D. J. Schuldt, Laura S. DeLuca, Kari Thomas, Taylor Berg-Kirkpatrick, Elizabeth Dieterich, Kartik Goyal, Max G'Sell

Issued in 1685, the Fourth Folio has been called "one of the most ineptly printed books published in the seventeenth century" (Hansen and Rasmussen 2017, 55). While this overlooks the shoddiness of presswork that prevailed in the period, some typographical flaws in the Folio do suggest a dogged carelessness in its printing. The title page of *Hamlet*, for instance, gives its leading role the nonsense honorific, "RPINCE OF DENMARK" (fig. 6.1). One likely reason for the Fourth Folio's at times muddled appearance is its collaborative making: it is a typographical hybrid, the product of three separate print shops working in tandem to bring a large book to market. That the Fourth Folio issued from three

---

Nikolai Vogler managed the machine learning pipeline and was the team's principal engineer. Christopher N. Warren led the project team and markedly improved the chapter during revisions. D. J. Schuldt wrote the section on our printer-publisher analysis and was responsible for identifying a majority of our candidate printers and books. Laura DeLuca contributed writing to the section on Robert Everingham. Kari Thomas, Elizabeth Dieterich, and D. J. Schuldt ensured our machine learning pipeline remained primed with candidate books. Kartik Goyal and Max G'Sell provided additional technical support, problem solving, and machine learning expertise. Nikolai Vogler, Kartik Goyal, Taylor Berg-Kirkpatrick, and Kari Thomas assisted in formatting and sourcing the figures. Research for this chapter was supported by grants from the National Science Foundation (*Print and Probability: A Statistical Approach to Analysis of Clandestine Publication*, NSF 1816311), XSEDE (HUM150002), and the National Endowment for the Humanities (*Freedom and the Press before Freedom of the Press: Tools, Data, and Methods for Researching Secret Printing*, HAA-284882–22).

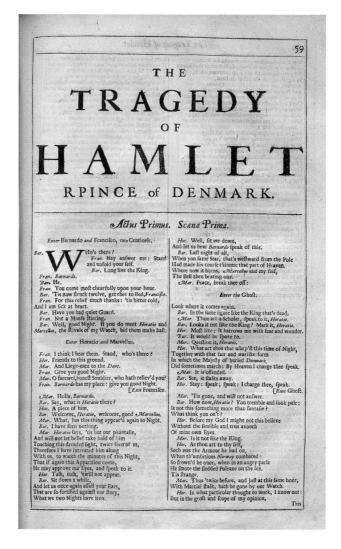

FIGURE 6.1 Hamlet, "RPINCE OF DENMARK" (Fourth Folio, 3E6r). Carnegie Mellon University Libraries, Special Collections, PR2751 .A4 1685.

presses has long been known. In his *Bibliography of the English Printed Drama to the Restoration*, W. W. Greg noted that the Fourth Folio "was divided into three sections for, presumably simultaneous, printing at different presses" (1962, 1120). Greg's three-printshop theory was based on the evidence of the three printers' types, and, in particular, on visual dissimilarities that segment the work into approximate thirds. The first printer's types and ornaments distinguish the first section, running from the Folio's title page through the comedies to the end of *The Winter's Tale* (sigs. π2, A1-Z4v, 1–274). The second (and longest) section—distinguished by a single decorative initial *N* and its printer's use of blackletter subtitles—opens with *The Life and Death of King John* and ends with *The Tragedy of Romeo and Juliet* (sigs. 2B-3E8v, 1–328). The third section, devoid of decorative initials, embraces the remainder of the tragedies beginning with *The Life of Timon of Athens* and runs through the apocryphal plays, ending with *The Tragedy of Locrine* (3A-4B8v, 1–304). Each section is also separately paginated, again reflecting the Folio's tripartite origin.

The Fourth Folio's collaborative making should not surprise us; the practice of shared printing was, according to Peter Blayney, "extremely common" in the early seventeenth century, and evidently continued to be so through the end of that century and beyond (Blayney 1973, 440). Shared printing allowed several print shops (or presses) to print concurrently, helping speed books to market. Such a practice meant a faster return on publishers' investments (The Fourth Folio was published by a consortium of four publishers; see Andrew Murphy's chapter in this volume). Although scholars have long recognized that the Fourth Folio was a collaborative undertaking, two of its three printers remain unknown. The Folio is only partially attributed in part because its printers' names are omitted from its title page. Unlike the First Folio of 1623 and the Second Folio of 1632 (whose title pages bear the names of their respective printers, Isaac Jaggard and Thomas Cotes, respectively), the Fourth Folio's three printers are left nameless, cloaked in an anonymity that has confounded scholars of Shakespeare's text for at least seven decades.

Greg's entry for the Fourth Folio in the *Bibliography of the English Printed Drama* cites a 1951 article by Fredson Bowers in attributing the first section to Robert Roberts (fl. 1679–1701): "The printer of the Comedies appears from the ornaments used to have been Robert Roberts, and he also printed the preliminaries. . . . The printer or printers of the later sections have not been identified" (1120). For his part, Bowers despaired of identifying the Folio's other printers and only tentatively assigned the title page—printed separately from the rest of the preliminaries on its own sheet of paper—to Roberts. While the Folio's second section offered useful, attributable evidence in the form of a single decorative initial *N*, Bowers failed to locate this same initial in any book printed in the period, leaving the question of its print shop unsettled: "the shop which produced . . . the second must await some fortunate discovery from the single initial" (Bowers 1951, 241). The third section was the most challenging. Bowers concluded that "the shop which produced the third section will perhaps never be identified until we know everything there is to be learned about seventeenth-century types" (241).

This chapter takes up Bowers's provocation and shows that the printers of the Fourth Folio's three sections were, respectively, Robert Roberts, Robert Everingham (fl. 1678–1700), and John Macock (fl. 1645–92). Rather than seeking typographical omniscience (who could achieve that?) we take a different

FIGURE 6.2   A digitally reconstructed broken uppercase *R* with its inked impression betraying a flaw in its piece of type. Carnegie Mellon University Libraries, Special Collections, PR2751 .A4 1685.

tack, employing computer vision and machine learning to sift, count, and categorize distinctively damaged types that appear in each of the Folio's three sections. While our tools are new, our aim is Bowers's own: to find distinctive types present in the unattributed sections of the Folio in other, attributed books printed circa 1685.

This method was termed "font analysis" by Adrian Weiss, but our focus on individual pieces of type ("sorts"), rather than entire fonts, makes "type analysis" nearer the mark. The logic behind this method is easily adduced (Weiss 1990, 122). Type sorts are metal objects, and in the course of their use (and reuse) in a seventeenth-century print shop, these objects suffered progressive and cumulative damage: types were dropped, trod on, hammered into place on the bed of the press, crushed, misused, and otherwise worn down by repeated contact with the press's heavy platen. Though metal, the special alloy used by typefounders of the period—a mixture of lead, antimony, and tin—was not especially durable. And so with repeated use, types degraded, effecting an atrophy consequent to printing type's primary function: repeatability. Evidence of this damage is visible in the inked impressions left by damaged sorts, as figure 6.2 shows.

No two pieces of type will degrade in precisely the same way. And so it follows that a distinctively battered piece of type—take, for example, the disfigured uppercase *R* in figure 6.2 that recurs in the Folio's second section—functions as an identifying characteristic of its printer, print shop, and case of type. Locating this same damaged *R* in another book printed in a known print shop would, in other words, reveal the identity of the printer of the Folio's second section. Damaged and distinctive types thus serve as a kind of typographical fingerprint: no two alike, they lay bare their respective origins. This fact allows us to trace the provenance of clandestinely or anonymously printed books whose printers have long evaded identification, as we have shown elsewhere (Warren et al. 2020, Goyal et al. 2020, Warren et al. 2021). The Fourth Folio, we theorized, would provide no exception.

The comparison and analysis of recurrent type sorts is an established practice of analytical bibliography, and it has been amply theorized and implemented by scholars, including Bowers, Blayney, Weiss, and Charlton Hinman. And for good reason: "A printer's type fonts," Weiss observed, "together with identifiable types, can be considered de facto proof of his [*sic*] identity" (1990, 96). Hinman, in *The Printing and Proof-Reading of the First Folio of Shakespeare* (1963), identified "600-odd individually distinctive types" that he traced through fifty-five copies of the First Folio. Modifying, and in some ways correcting, Hinman's work, Blayney outstripped this mark, finding 2131 appearances of 571 distinctive types in his study of a single play, the 1608 quarto edition of *King Lear*—this in addition to hundreds of factotums (decorative frames designed to hold individual pieces of metal type), printers' flowers, woodcut ornaments, and titling letters (Blayney 1982, 432–539).

Our method updates that of Weiss, Blayney, Hinman and others through our use of computation. Primarily, we worked not from a physical copy of the Fourth Folio, but from a high-resolution digital facsimile made by scanning a copy held in Carnegie Mellon University Special Collections and encoding the resulting page images as .tiff (Tag Image File Format) files. Running these images through our machine-learning pipeline yielded a set of more than twenty-five thousand distinctively damaged characters. To tame this trove, we focused our attention on sixteen uppercase letters (ABCDEFGHKLMNPRTW), choosing these letters, in particular, for their size and form (uppercase, heavily serifed letters seem to accrue more damages, and their added height helped us perceive minute features that might otherwise be overlooked on more compact lowercase sorts). The result was a vast and strange alphabet of bent *W*s, shabby *D*s, bow-legged *H*s, and nicked *C*s (fig. 6.3). We then turned to gathering a list of candidate books for comparison—a corpus comprising a subset of all books printed in London within ten years of the Folio's publication. This comparison set was also (and out of necessity, given our workflow) made up of digital facsimiles, many of which have only recently been made available via online repositories, such as

FIGURE 6.3   Damaged type algorithmically harvested from the Fourth Folio. Carnegie Mellon University Libraries, Special Collections, PR2751 .A4 1685.

HathiTrust, Gallica, and Internet Archive. Others were sourced from smaller, institutional repositories, such as those maintained by the British Library and Folger Shakespeare Library.

This sea change in the quantity (and format) of evidence tractable for computational analysis is transformative, not least because its form—printed pages rendered as digital files—has created the opportunity for a kind of inquiry that differs from classical font analysis in degree if not in kind. However, bibliographers have been slow to recognize the evidence latent in scanned books, a byproduct perhaps of analytical bibliography's ingrained distrust of photographic reproduction, which always "obscures what it reproduces" (W. W. Greg quoted in Tanselle 1989, 25). This point of view reflects the perceived and real limitations of earlier technologies, such as microfilm and xerography, that were (and are) inadequate for the fine-grained analysis of bibliographical evidence. Yet modern high-resolution cameras make this blanket distrust of reproductions seem increasingly outdated.

There are signs of new thinking, however. Sarah Werner imagines a future in which scans of Shakespeare Folios will be examined by "computer script" and suggests that "we are moving toward a time when digital facsimiles are going to be seen as digital objects in their own right: not as surrogates for a printed book . . . but as different ways to experience that object." Werner concludes with a prediction that "for some uses, the material text might be better suited; for others, a digital image might be a better choice" (Werner 2016, 182). Modifying this point, Zachary Lesser and Whitney Trettien argue for a "bibliographic approach to the digital facsimile that acknowledges both its independence from and its close, functional relationship to the material text that it aims to reproduce" (Lesser and Trettien 2021, 418). Our work, which relies on the computational analysis of digital copies of early printed books, represents one step in this direction. In similar terms, Jeffrey Todd Knight sees in Shakespeare studies a turn toward "computational or quantitative approaches" that rely on "emergent tools" (Knight 2017, 8). Ryan Cordell meanwhile proposes a new type of bibliographical inquiry based on an "experimental approach to the digitised archive." Dubbed speculative bibliography, Cordell's approach "weaves together textual editing and computational speculation." Implicit in Werner's, Knight's, and Cordell's writing is the idea that a bibliography of digital images and text is inevitable: new tools and methods are needed to make use of vast bodies of evidence, much of it lodged in digital formats.

New tools are also needed to improve upon existing methods. The type and font analysis developed by analytical bibliographers is hampered by its difficulty, a fact even its principal theorists acknowledged. Weiss admitted that font analysis is a "devastatingly tedious task" (Weiss 1991, 185). Hinman was even less sanguine, describing collation (i.e., the process of comparing copies of the same edition) as "one of the most arduous and time-consuming of all possible bibliographical activities—and often . . . one of the dullest" (Hinman 1947, 100). Hinman's position didn't change with time. Sixteen years later, he wrote that collation and type analysis require "continuous attention to very small matters—among other things to the almost infinitely various 'patterns' in which hundreds of individual types appear and reappear in different parts of the Folio" (Hinman 1963, 12). While Hinman was here writing about the First Folio, the Fourth presents comparable difficulties. The Fourth contains more than 3.2 million letters, each at least potentially made by a distinctively damaged piece of type. Hinman's Dantean warning given at the end of his introduction to *The Printing and Proofreading* still rings true: "From some complexity, at least, the evidence itself allows no escape" (Hinman 1963, 14).

Hinman's solution was technological. The analysis of typographical evidence in the First Folio "had been made possible," Hinman wrote, "by . . . the perfecting of an optical instrument which greatly facilitates the collation of any given book" (Hinman 1963, 7). Eight years before, Hinman had announced the invention of this "optical instrument"—a device eventually named the "Hinman collator"—in a short article: "The new collating machine makes the bibliographical exploitation of [a] vast body of material possible for the first time" (Hinman 1955, 134). Hinman's instrument-aided analysis, which he called "mechanized collation," proved influential; several Hinman collators are still functional, including one held in Carnegie Mellon University Libraries Special Collections (fig. 6.4).

There is a rich tradition, then, flowing through Hinman, that uses instruments and technology to examine early printed editions of Shakespeare's plays. In prototyping and developing instruments of our own, we participate in this tradition, offering a computational analog to Hinman's mechanized collator—one

FIGURE 6.4 A functioning Hinman Collator held in Carnegie Mellon University Libraries, Special Collections. Photo by Samuel V. Lemley.

that delivers on Hinman's promise of a tool for discerning "the almost infinitely various 'patterns' in which . . . individual types" recur.

Our algorithms operate by deconstructing a digitized page into its most basic constituent parts: individual pieces of type. First, our computational toolkit automatically segments page scans into their constituent columns of text. These columns of text are then segmented into their constituent lines, which are then segmented into their constituent letters. These isolated letters are classified with OCR (Optical Character Recognition) and assessed for damage against a synthetic, idealized letterform—a visual average of non-damaged characters of the same sort. The farther a letter departs from this ideal model, the higher its "damage score." A bent and fractured uppercase *F*, for instance, will be assigned a higher damage score compared to an uppercase *F* that is unbent and unfractured.

This amounts to a new kind of bibliographical analysis that we call *computational bibliography* (Warren et al. 2021). Computers make the emergent glut of digital bibliographical evidence tractable. Uniquely suited to the rote mechanics of pattern recognition and variant detection, they spot evidence that is either imperceptible or only laboriously perceived by human eyes. But we hasten to add that our tools are the product of trial and error, innovative tinkering, and a bootstrapped ethos. For all their transformative promise, these tools do not (yet) allow us to avoid problems common to traditional bibliographical analysis, including, for instance, the gathering of a set of books for analysis and comparison—a problem we turn to in the next section.

GATHERING A COMPARISON SET: PUBLISHER-PRINTER ANALYSIS

Unlike the computational gathering of distinctive types, curating a set of attributed books for analysis was far from automatic. In 1684 and 1685—the years in which Fourth Folio was most likely at press—there were roughly eighty printers at work in the city of London. The ideal candidate set for comparison, then, would comprise eighty attributed books printed in pica roman—the same font size used in the Folio, twenty lines of which measure approximately eighty-one millimeters in height (Gaskell 1995, 15). However, several problems emerged when we set out to curate this comparison set. First, during this period, printers evidently used pica roman less often than the larger "english" size (twenty lines of which measure approximately ninety-two millimeters), and so our search for books containing pica types for each of our candidate printers was impeded by scarcity. Another set of challenges stemmed from the fact that we were working with digital facsimiles: Had enough books printed in pica been digitized, much less at an adequate resolution? Also—and perhaps more fundamentally—how would we determine the size of a typeface from a digital facsimile? Absent any indication of scale, a digitally rendered "english" roman is indistinguishable from a digitally rendered pica. Of the hundreds of books printed in London in 1684/5, we only needed to find three in theory, but we needed to find three very specific needles in a haystack—or rather several haystacks—held in libraries around the world.

The first step was to narrow the candidate list of printers to those that had the greatest likelihood of providing matches to the distinctive types we had extracted from the Fourth Folio. Our foundational assumption was that the Folio was a large enough project that it was unlikely that its publishers would choose a printer (or printers) with whom they had no prior experience. Apart from the motives of economy and productive capacity, Philip Gaskell noted that "printing may occasionally have been split up . . . in order to share out work equitably between the members of a partnership or the various owners of a copyright" (1995, 168). Using data from the English Short Title Catalogue (ESTC), we created a list of candidates made up primarily of printers who were printing in 1684/5 and who had previously printed for any of Folio's original publishers—Henry Herringman, Edward Brewster, Richard Bentley, and Robert Chiswell—or its booksellers—Joseph Knight and Francis Saunders. With the addition of a couple printers of interest for other reasons (including Roberts, who apparently had never printed for the Folio's publishers, but to whom Bowers had attributed the Folio's first section), we narrowed the maximum list of approximately eighty potential candidates down to eleven printers (with the years they were actively printing):

- Joseph Bennet, 1674–91
- Mary Clark, 1677–96
- John Darby, 1667–1704
- Robert Everingham, 1678–1700
- John Gain, 1680–87
- Henry Hills, Jr., 1683–1713
- Thomas Hodkins, 1677–1713
- John Macock, 1645–92
- Thomas Newcomb, Jr., 1681–91
- William Rawlins, 1667–1707
- Robert Roberts, 1679–1701

Some of these printers were well-connected with our group of publishers and printers. John Macock, for example, printed for Herringman at least eighteen times between 1675 and 1684. Robert Everingham—a former apprentice of Macock's—had only set up shop in the late 1670s, but by 1684 he had printed for both Chiswell and Bentley.

Our initial hope was that compiling a list of candidate printers would be the difficult part. This was not the case. We succeeded in finding high-quality scans of books printed by these printers in various online repositories, but we specifically needed books that contained pica roman types in sufficient quantities. While the ESTC does include a great deal of information about early English books, there is no comparable database that records the dimensions of the typefaces used in a particular edition. How, then, does one determine the size of a typeface from a digital facsimile? The standard method for determining font size is to measure twenty lines of text in millimeters and to compare that measurement to known averages—for instance, those recorded in Gaskell's table of "Names and Body-sizes of Text Types in the Hand-press Period," which provides a range of heights for each font size in different historical periods (Gaskell 1995, 15). Some digitized books have been photographed with rulers, which allowed us to measure fonts directly on screen. However, the vast majority of digitized books do not include a photographed ruler, and so the point is moot.

Though we are currently at work on a computational method for determining font size on scanned pages, that tool is not yet ready for implementation. We therefore pieced together a workable method using three different data points. First, we hand-measured books that we had physical access to, which gave us an (admittedly small) set of extremely reliable data. Second, we used this dataset to infer font size based on the number of lines of text per page relative to the book's format (i.e., folio, quarto, octavo). For example, our data showed that a quarto printed in pica would have a lines-per-page (LPP) count of between forty and forty-seven, with a smaller range of forty-two to forty-five LPP increasing the likelihood. Unsurprisingly, this method proved to be less reliable than hand-measurement but was still a useful diagnostic tool. Third, we found Early English Books Online (EEBO) scans to be helpful in this area. EEBO scans are usually inadequate for detecting damaged types, but there are many EEBO scans that include rulers, usually photographed among the frontmatter, that allowed us to measure twenty-line segments reliably.

Once we had a way to estimate the size of types in digitized books, we still needed to find books printed in pica by our eleven candidate printers that were close enough in time to 1685 that they might contain the damaged types evident in the Fourth Folio. Though the closer to 1685 the better, the date range of candidate books was necessarily extended beyond 1684 and 1685, given that there is no guarantee that the Folio's anonymous printers printed other works with the same types used in the Folio during these years; nor, for that matter, any guarantee that these hypothetical books would have survived to the present *and* be available in a digital format. To expand our historical frame, we focused on gathering books printed by our eleven candidate printers within ten years of 1685—that is, between 1675 and 1695.

By narrowing the candidate list, determining typeface sizes, and then gathering examples of books in pica from each candidate printer from a period of ten years before and ten years after 1685, we found matches for all three sections of the Folio. "Gathering" is, of course, a generous term, implying a bounty of evidence. In truth, only a fraction of extant editions published in London during this twenty-year span have been digitized at a suitable resolution. Despite this, there are hundreds of digitized books available online (a number that grows daily), which allowed us to amass an adequate corpus for comparison. Some particularly promising candidates unavailable on existing online repositories were scanned on request and added to our machine learning pipeline. Still, we can look forward to a future in which more of the printed record is available in digital format.

In the end, we examined hundreds of books printed between 1675 and 1695 to build our candidate book list. Some candidates were easier to find than others. For example, we examined twenty-five books printed by Mary Clark and found four candidate books printed in pica. We examined thirty-one books printed by Robert Everingham but only turned up two in pica. Running the books gathered for each of our eleven candidate printers through our machine learning pipeline revealed that Everingham printed the second section and Macock printed the third; our analysis also confirmed Bowers's attribution of the first section, including the preliminaries, to Roberts. We detail the typographical evidence that forms the basis of these attributions in the following sections.

PART AND PRINTER ONE: ROBERT ROBERTS

Bowers assigned the first section of the Fourth Folio to Roberts on the basis of a set of "somewhat crudely cut" floriated initials (Bowers 1951, 241). These initials make up a partial alphabet of large white-body letters superimposed on floral and vegetal patterns. Each of the first section's fourteen plays opens with one of these crudely cut initials, with the same initial *I* recurring six times. Bowers found the same floriated initial *B* that opens the Folio's *The Tempest* in a 1677 edition of Beaumont and Fletcher's *The Scornful Lady* (ESTC R24847, fig. 6.5). The title page of *Scornful Lady* names two printers, however—Anne Maxwell and Robert Roberts—leaving the ownership of the initials open to doubt: Were they Roberts's or Maxwell's? A second book, printed solely by Roberts in 1699, seemed to settle the issue: "To clinch the case . . . the initial *N* found for Midsummer Night's Dream on sig. L4v of the [Fourth] Folio appears in Walter Harris, *A Description of the King's Royal Palace and Gardens at Loo*" (Bowers 1951, 243; ESTC R6026). On the basis of this evidence, Bowers inferred that the initials belonged to Roberts alone.

A caveat accompanies the attribution of the first section of the Fourth Folio to Roberts, however: Bowers did not find categorical proof that Roberts alone owned the floriated initials in 1684 and 1685, the years in which the Folio was likely printed. The fact that these initials appear in a book co-printed by Roberts and Maxwell in 1677 suggests that they might have belonged instead to Maxwell, a possibility Bowers dismissed based on evidence in the Stationers' Register. After May 1682, the Register—a record book in which publishers entered their rights to print specific works—lists no books entered by or for Anne Maxwell. This suggested to Bowers that the Maxwell-Roberts partnership had dissolved by May 1683, when Roberts began to print books alone, and when Maxwell "was

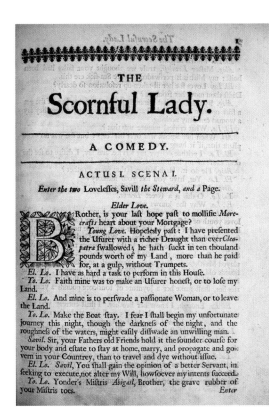
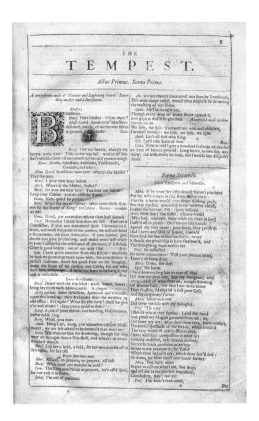

FIGURE 6.5   *Left*: The "crudely-cut floral initial" *B* in *Scornful Lady* (1677), "demonstrably the same as that which opens the Tempest" in the Fourth Folio, according to Bowers. *Right*: The same initial *B* on page 1 of the Fourth Folio. *Left*: Boston Public Library, G.3966.12 no.4; *right*: Carnegie Mellon University Libraries, Special Collections, PR2751 .A4 1685.

either retired or dead." The last book co-printed by Maxwell and Roberts that Bowers succeeded in identifying was John Collinges's *The History of Conformity*, printed in 1681 (ESTC R28566). Any appearance of the floriated initials after this date could therefore be ascribed to Roberts. If the floriated initials *had* belonged to Maxwell, Bowers reasoned, they evidently passed to Roberts after her death or retirement.

New evidence modifies Bowers account, however. The ESTC lists nine Maxwell-Roberts books that post-date the *History of Conformity*: three books printed in 1682 (ESTC R19305, R219414, R34621), three books printed in 1683 (ESTC R170099, R180051, R493042), and three books printed in 1684 (ESTC R186613, R171518, R11740). Among the three 1684 editions co-printed by Maxwell and Roberts is the second volume of *The Works of the Late Learned Divine Stephen Charnock* (ESTC R11740). Charnock's *Works* contains the floriated initials that appear in the first section of the Fourth Folio, including its six-time recurrent initial *I*.

This undermines Bowers's conjecture that the floriated initials were in Roberts's sole possession after 1682. Absent a pre-1684 edition printed by Roberts alone with the floriated initials, the possibility remains that Maxwell owned the initials up to that date. We failed to find such an edition.

Although Anne Maxwell did not die in 1682/83, Bowers's account is otherwise sound: Roberts evidently began printing alone in 1684, while in the same year Maxwell's output and activity waned. Meanwhile, the presence of the floriated initials in *A Description of the King's Royal Palace and Gardens at Loo*—a book Roberts printed alone—indicates that Roberts owned the initials after Maxwell's cessation of business or death in 1684. It follows, then, that the appearance of these initials in the first section of the Folio supports an assignment to Roberts.

Still, doubts remain. Printers' ornaments of all kinds—decorative headpieces (printed at the start, or "head" of book chapters or sections), tailpieces, borders, and initials, usually cut in blocks of wood, though sometimes cast or cut in metal plates that were nailed onto wood blocks—are of questionable merit in attributing anonymously printed books. As Peter Blayney has observed, "printers were in the habit of borrowing each others' ornaments," and besides this, ornaments were sold and produced in multiples, copied, or otherwise imitated (Blayney 1982, 36). Ornaments that lack any identifying damage or other characteristic mark are easily confused with imitations or copies of the same design. Tentative attributions can be made based on the occurrence of an ornament of known provenance. But, as Weiss has suggested, these speculative attributions should be confirmed by more rigorous font analysis and identification.

While the decorative initials in the first section of the Folio imply, then, that Roberts was responsible for its printing, we were left wanting further evidence. Pieces of type can strengthen attributions. Seventeenth-century type sorts, like ornaments, were also manufactured in multiples—each letter cast in thousands from the same mold. But the damages these sorts accrued in casting or in use are characteristic and, in large numbers, distinctive enough to be used in identifying their typecase, print shop, and printer. We found such typographical evidence to confirm Bowers's attribution of the first section of the Folio to Roberts in William Poole's *Annotations Upon the Holy Bible*, a large folio printed in 1688 (fig. 6.6). Crucially, Roberts is the only printer named in the imprint on the title page of the *Annotations*, and therefore we can be reasonably certain he printed the book alone.

Several distinctively damaged letters appear on the title page of Poole's *Annotations*. Among these are the *L* and the *Y* in HO<u>LY</u>, both visibly marred. The *L*'s leg is fractured, its upper serif bent and broken, and the righthand edge

FIGURE 6.6   Title page, *Annotations upon the Holy Bible* (London: Robert Roberts, 1688), showing the distinctively damaged *L* and *Y* in HO<u>LY</u> unique to Robert Roberts. Carnegie Mellon University Libraries, Special Collections.

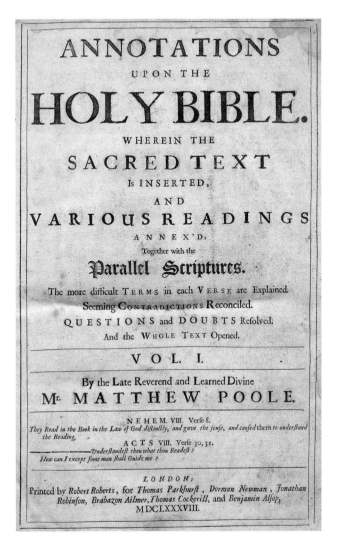

of its trunk nicked and cracked. The *Y* is similarly disfigured, with several nicks visible on both of its arms (fig. 6.8). These same letters appear on two (of three extant) states of the Folio's title page in the word P<u>LA</u>YS (fig. 6.7). The three versions, or "states" of the title page are distinguished by their imprints. One names Herringman, Brewster, and Bentley as its publishers; the second adds Chiswell to this list; and the third names Herringman as its publisher, as well as Knight and Saunders as deputized booksellers. The title pages bearing the first two imprints—that is, both states that do not name Knight and Saunders—have the distinctive *L* and *Y* in the word P<u>LA</u>YS. Under magnification, the similarities are unmistakable, demonstrating that these four printed characters derived from the same two pieces of type (fig. 6.8). Especially revealing are scattered

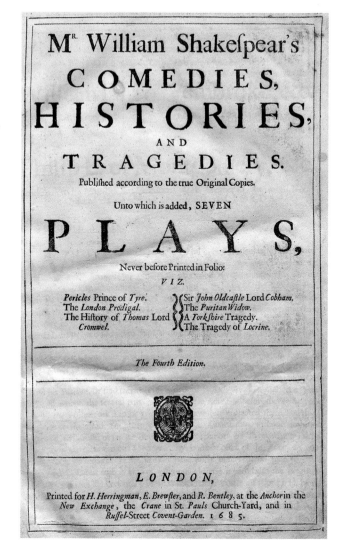

FIGURE 6.7 Fourth Folio title page, *Mr. William Shakespear's Comedies, Histories, and Tragedies*, showing the distinctively damaged *L* and *Y* in PLAYS that appear in figure 6.6. Carnegie Mellon University Libraries, Special Collections, PR2751 .A4 1685.

flecks of type metal or debris near the lower half of the damaged *Y*. In both the 1688 *Annotations* and the Fourth Folio, these flecks took ink and left discernible marks in identical positions (fig. 6.9). The dimensions of each pair are also identical—twenty millimeters in height.

We identified these matching letters using traditional font analysis unaided by computational tools. Computational bibliography, such as it is, is as yet an imperfect science. In this case, we failed to locate a digital scan of a Roberts book printed in the same pica roman body type as the first section of the Folio. Consequently, we were unable to compare Roberts's Fourth Folio pica font with an approximately contemporary sample from another Roberts book. Despite this, the attribution of the Folio's first section to Roberts is incontrovertible: in combination with the floriated initials assigned to Roberts by Bowers, the damaged *L* and *Y* amount to proof that Robert Roberts printed the first section of the Fourth Folio, including the preliminaries as well as two states of the title page. The third state of the title page, with Knight and Saunders named in the imprint, was printed by John Macock, as we show in a later section.

FIGURE 6.8 The distinctively damaged *L* and *Y* as printed on the title page of William Poole, *Annotations Upon the Holy Bible* (*top*) and as printed on the title page of the Fourth Folio (*bottom*). Carnegie Mellon University Libraries, Special Collections.

FIGURE 6.9 Inked flecks of type metal or debris visible in both impressions of the damaged *Y*: Fourth Folio (*left*); *Annotations* (*right*). Carnegie Mellon University Libraries, Special Collections.

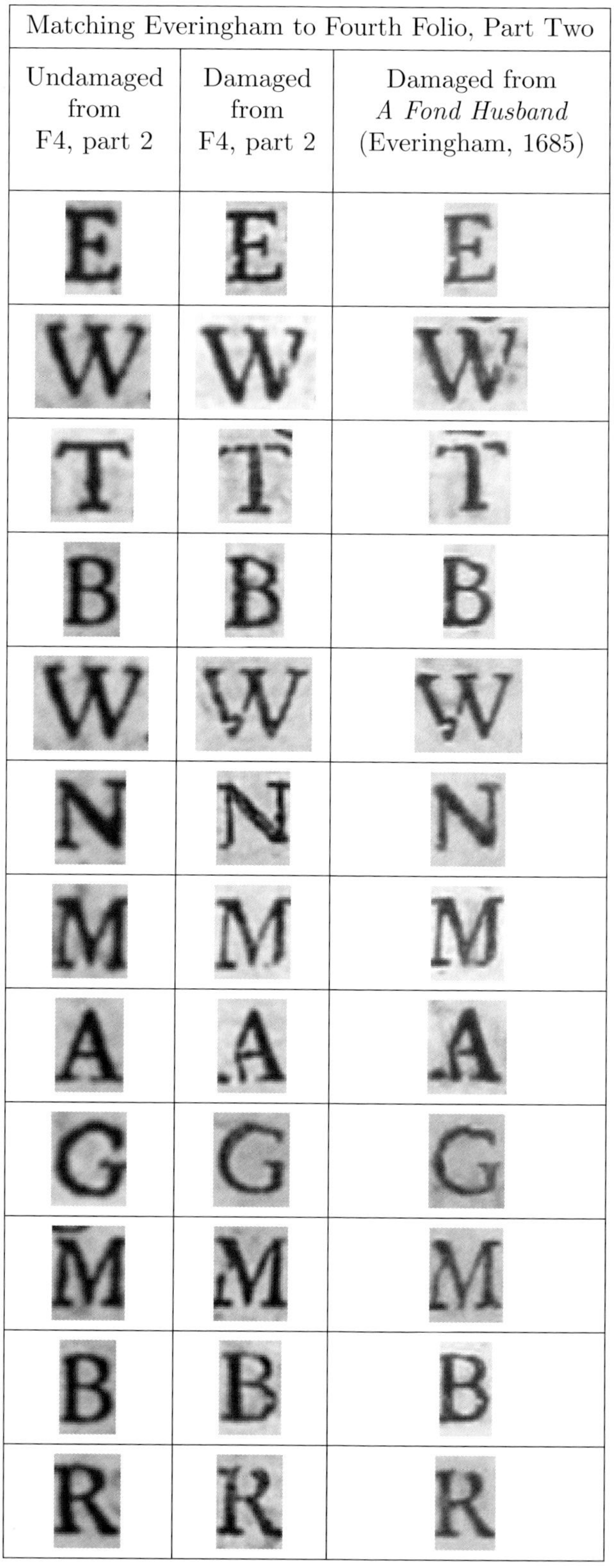

FIGURE 6.10 A table showing Fourth Folio-to-Everingham matches found in Everingham's *A Fond Husband* (ESTC R15791). © British Library Board, 644.h.16.

Matching Everingham to Fourth Folio, Part Two		
Undamaged from F4, part 2	Damaged from F4, part 2	Damaged from *A Fond Husband* (Everingham, 1685)
E	E	E
W	W	W
T	T	T
B	B	B
W	W	W
N	N	N
M	M	M
A	A	A
G	G	G
M	M	M
B	B	B
R	R	R

PART AND PRINTER TWO: ROBERT EVERINGHAM

Bowers maintained that the Fourth Folio's second section would only be attributed by the chance discovery of its sole decorative initial—a five-line, white-body *N*—in another book printed by a known printer in the period. Despairing of accidental detection, we opted for exhaustive analysis, finding several compelling matches for damaged letters that recur in the second section of the Folio in Thomas D'Urfey's *A Fond Husband: or, the Plotting Sisters, a Comedy* (ESTC R15791), printed in 1685 by Robert Everingham.

Among the most persuasive matches found in *A Fond Husband* is a distinctively damaged uppercase *A*. Its left leg is severed at an oblique angle, and the remaining type metal is bent inward toward the *A*'s right leg (see fig. 6.10, row eight). Both damaged impressions also appear to show an identical break where the bar meets the severed left diagonal, although the break is obscured by heavy inking in the Folio impression. An array of other matches found in *Fond Husband* are comparably persuasive. These include an uppercase *B* with an oddly shaped bowl dented on its upper edge (fig. 6.10, row four), an uppercase *T* with two breaks in its horizontal bar (fig. 6.10, row three), and an uppercase *W* with a distinctive, nearly encysted bend in its left joint (fig. 6.10, row five). Many of the damaged types found in *A Fond Husband* defy description, but their kinship to similarly damaged sorts in the Folio is demonstrated visually in figure 6.10. In total, figure 6.10 shows twelve convincingly matched pairs of uppercase letters found in both *A Fond Husband* and the Fourth Folio, demonstrating that Everingham printed the second section of the Folio alone.

PART AND PRINTER 3: JOHN MACOCK

The third section of the Fourth Folio contains no printers' ornaments, so any effort to identify its printer and print shop is limited to the evidence of its types. In contrast to Roberts's numerous floriated initials in the first section, for instance, the third section marks the beginning of each of its fifteen plays with unadorned titling letters (fig. 6.1). Apart from their size, these letters closely resemble the uppercase letters found in the adjacent body text. Absent, too, from the third section are printers' flowers, or *fleurons*—small, cast-in-metal ornaments designed to be set in-line with type. Bowers viewed what remained of the typographical evidence as a kind of void: types unaccompanied by ornamental stock offered little traction for analysis and few leads. To attribute the third section would require attributing its fonts, and such a task, Bowers concluded in a phrase we have quoted already, demanded nothing short of "learning everything there is to know about seventeenth-century types."

Instead, we discovered that our publisher-printer analysis provided a narrower scope than Bowers anticipated. From the whole of seventeenth-century type evidence, we winnowed out eleven likely printers. Working with this shortlist of candidates, our machine learning pipeline returned several distinctive types in the Folio's third section, all of which pointed to printer John Macock (1645–1692). Two Macock books in particular provided the bulk of these matches: Theophilus Gale's *The Court of the Gentiles* (ESTC R25438) and George Etheredge's *The Man of Mode, or, Sr Fopling Flutter* (ESTC R25438). A third Macock book, book 3 of part 4 of *The Court of the Gentiles* (ESTC R16919), printed in 1678, provided another three matches. Though not attributed to Macock on the title page, internal matches to Macock's 1677 *Court of the Gentiles* volume (ESTC R25438) confirmed that he also printed the 1678 volume.

One of the most convincing Macock-to-Folio matches is an uppercase *W* that recurs in the third section of the Folio and in part 4 of Theophilus Gale's *The Court of the Gentiles*, printed in 1677 by Macock (ESTC R25438). The right arm (or fourth diagonal) of the *W* is broken, and both of its serifs incline inward (fig. 6.11, row seven). Several other letters that appear in both the third section of the Folio and books printed by John Macock in 1684, are similarly convincing. These include a stubbed-toe uppercase *K*, a fractured uppercase *C*, and an uppercase *A* with a broken and bent left diagonal that ends in an anemic serif (fig. 6.11).

Given their proximity in time to the Fourth Folio, matches found in *Man of Mode*—printed in 1684, just a year before the Folio—are in some ways more convincing, and we expected to prefer them over matches found in Macock's 1677 *Court of Gentiles*. However, we were surprised to find that identifiable types in *Court of Gentiles* were often nearly identical to their counterparts in the Folio, despite the years that intervened. This suggests that even profoundly damaged type sorts were kept in use in Macock's print shop for at least six years, and likely much longer. Though this might be explained by the fact that Macock printed in pica roman only infrequently, it still contradicts the scholarly consensus that damaged types were often recycled, replenished, or replaced on a comparatively short cycle. This is even more striking given the conditions that prevailed in Macock's shop. As Plomer's *Dictionary of the Booksellers and Printers 1641–1667* notes, a survey of London printers conducted in 1668 showed that Macock then had "three presses, three apprentices and ten workmen; it was, in fact, one of the largest printing houses in London" (Plomer 1907, 121). We can assume that Macock's stock of type was proportionate, and that his types saw a good deal of use in the period 1677–85. All of which suggests that damaged or otherwise imperfect types were tolerated and retained for a period of time longer than we

| Matching Macock to Fourth Folio, Part Three |||||
Undamaged from F4, part 3	Damaged from F4, part 3	Damaged from *Court of the Gentiles* (Macock, 1677)	Damaged from *Court of the Gentiles* ([Macock], 1678)	Damaged from *Man of Mode* (Macock, 1685)
W	W		W	
M	M	M		
N	N			N
L	L		L	
C	C			C
A	A	A		
W	W	W		
T	T			T
K	K		K	

FIGURE 6.11 A table of distinctively damaged types that appear in part 3 of the Fourth Folio; George Etheredge's *The Man of Mode, or, Sr Fopling Flutter* (ESTC R25438) (PR3432 .A67 1684, by permission of Woodson Research Center, Fondren Library, Rice University); and part 4, book 2 (ESTC R25438) and book 3 (ESTC R16919) of Theophilus Gale's *The Court of the Gentiles* (Special Collections, Wright Library, Princeton Theological Seminary Library, SCC 9015).

predicted, a finding that bodes well for scholars seeking recurrences of type separated by many years.

Yet these Macock-to-Folio body type matches are less numerous and somehow less convincing than those we found for Everingham, leaving our attribution on shaky ground. A final piece of evidence confirmed our attribution of the

Folio's third section to Macock, however. After computationally extracting all of the large, multiline titling letters that appear in Macock books on the Early English Books Online (EEBO) database, we used our machine learning pipeline to seek out matches for comparably sized letters that appear in the Folio's third section. Doing so yielded several convincing pairs. For instance, we found a distinctive *R* that recurs in the word TRAGEDY in the third section's play titles in a number of Macock books. In each case, the same peculiar notch appears where the *R*'s legs join (fig. 6.12). This *R* appears in Beaumont and Fletcher's *Fifty Comedies and Tragedies*, printed by Macock and Henry Hills in 1679 (ESTC R13766); in *A Paraphrase and Annotations Upon All the Books of the New Testament*, printed by Macock and Miles Flesher in 1681 (ESTC R5975); and in Jeremy Taylor's *Eniautos, A Course of Sermons*, printed by Macock alone in 1678 (ESTC R1244).

Similarly, we found the distinctively damaged *Y* that ends the word PLAY in the title of *Pericles* in the third section of the Fouth Folio on the title page of *The History of the Life and Death of the Holy Jesus* (Part 2), printed by Macock in 1683 (fig. 6.13). The 1683 *Holy Jesus* impression, though obscured by EEBO's origins in microfilm, shows the same bends and nicks as appear in the *Y* in the Folio: its left foot curls upward, the outer edge of its upper left serif resembles an errant strand of hair, and an odd protuberance juts from the left-hand side of its trunk. This same *Y* also appears on the state of the Folio's title page that names Knight and Saunders in the imprint, demonstrating that Macock was responsible not only for the third section of the Folio's text, but also one state of its title page (fig. 6.14).

FIGURE 6.12 A distinctively damaged titling *R* that appears in every instance, save one, of the word TRAGEDY in play titles of the Fourth Folio's third section (*left*: Carnegie Mellon University Libraries, Special Collections, PR2751 .A4 1685). This same *R* was found in Beaumont and Fletcher, *Fifty Comedies and Tragedies* (London: J[ohn]. Macock [Henry Hills], 1679; ESTC R13766) (*middle left*: Carnegie Mellon University Libraries, Special Collections, PR2420 1679); *A Paraphrase and Annotations Upon All the Books of the New Testament* (London: J[ohn]. Macock and M[iles]. Flesher, 1681; ESTC R5975) (*middle right*: The Huntington Library, 434526); and Jeremy Taylor, *Eniautos* (London: J[ohn]. Macock, 1678; ESTC R1244) (*right*: The Rare Book & Manuscript Library, University of Illinois at Urbana-Champaign, XQ 252 .T215E1678).

FIGURE 6.13   A distinctively damaged titling *Y* that appears in both the title of the Fourth Folio *Pericles* (*left*: Carnegie Mellon University Libraries, Special Collections, PR2751 .A4 1685) and part 2 of *The History of the Life and Death of the Holy Jesus* (London: J[ohn]. Macock for R[ichard]. Royston, 1683; ESTC R217592) (*middle*: The Rare Book & Manuscript Library, University of Illinois at Urbana-Champaign, IUQ04156). It also appears on the Knight-Saunders setting of the Fourth Folio title page (*right*: Boston Public Library, Special Collections, G.176.4 FOLIO).

THE FIFTH FOLIO (1700); OR, ROBERT EVERINGHAM REDUX

In 1952, Giles Dawson, then working at the Folger Shakespeare Library in Washington DC, noticed several irregularities in the Fourth Folio's printing. Most conspicuously, some copies contained seventeen reprinted sheets (or sixty-eight pages) interpolated in the second section. Dawson located the reprinted sheets in only six copies of the Folio, though he also found evidence of emendation: incidental errors had been corrected in the reprinted sheets and the spelling modernized ("*will* for *wil*, *Doll.* for *Dol.*, *Country* for *Countrey*, *warlike* for *warlick*, *Lion* for *Lyon*") to fit an orthographic trend he located somewhat imprecisely in "the last decades of the seventeenth century and the early years of the eighteenth" (Dawson 1952, 98). Dawson's conjectural date for the reprinted sheets, 1700, has been confirmed by Laura Hansen and Eric Rasmussen (2017, 55–62). In other words, the reprinted and corrected sheets postdated the Fourth Folio by fifteen years.

The circumstances of the printing of these seventeen sheets are unknown. The standing theory is that when, in 1698, Richard Bentley sold his share in the copyright of Shakespeare's plays to Richard Wellington, Wellington received Bentley's unsold copies of the Fourth Folio unbound and in sheets. On or shortly after receiving these copies, Wellington found them deficient; the printer of the second section had short-sheeted his portion of the work (Hansen and Rasmussen 2017; Mandelbrote 1997; Belanger 1975). Naturally eager to avoid the sale of incomplete copies, Wellington had the missing sheets reprinted, correcting Everingham's fifteen-year-old error.

Though not properly belonging to the Fourth Folio (Dawson strained the bibliographical distinction between edition, issue, and state and called them "F5

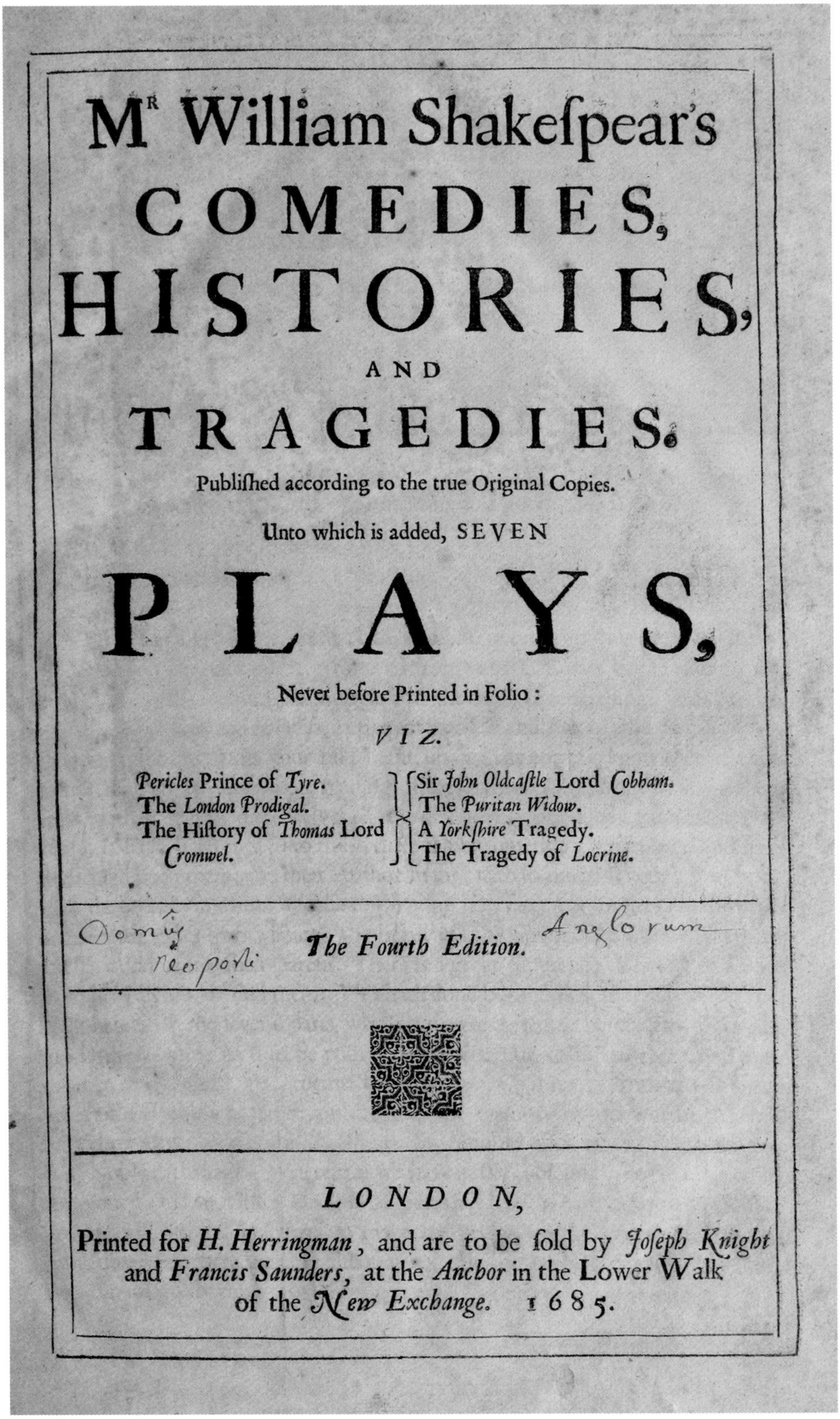

Mr William Shakespear's
COMEDIES,
HISTORIES,
AND
TRAGEDIES.

Published according to the true Original Copies.

Unto which is added, SEVEN

PLAYS,

Never before Printed in Folio:

VIZ.

Pericles Prince of *Tyre*. } { Sir *John Oldcastle* Lord *Cobham*.
The *London* Prodigal.   } { The *Puritan* Widow.
The History of *Thomas* Lord } { A *Yorkshire* Tragedy.
Cromwel.   } { The Tragedy of *Locrine*.

Domũs   **The Fourth Edition.**   *Anglorum*
Neopoli

LONDON,

Printed for *H. Herringman*, and are to be sold by *Joseph Knight* and *Francis Saunders*, at the *Anchor* in the Lower Walk of the *New* Exchange. 1685.

FIGURE 6.14   The Knight-Saunders state of the Fourth Folio's title page, showing the distinctively damaged *Y* shown in figure 6.13. Boston Public Library, G.176.4 FOLIO.

FIGURE 6.15 Matches in the Fourth Folio part 2 (printed by Everingham) and the reprinted "Fifth Folio" sheets. Folger Shakespeare Library, S2915 Fo.4 no.28, and S2915 Fo.4 no.33.

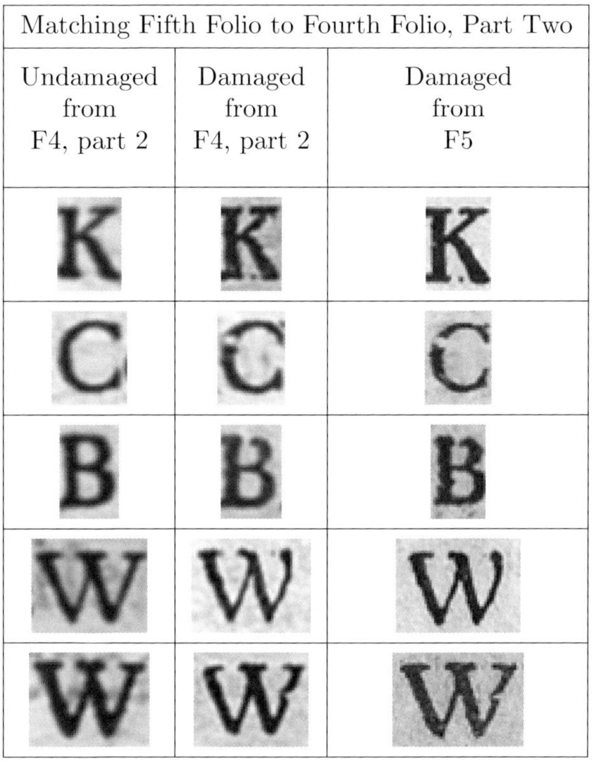

Matching Fifth Folio to Fourth Folio, Part Two		
Undamaged from F4, part 2	Damaged from F4, part 2	Damaged from F5
K	K	K
C	C	C
B	B	B
W	W	W
W	W	W

[the Fifth Folio], since they constitute a fifth folio printing"), these reprinted sheets serve only to complicate the problem of the Fourth's attribution: they represent yet another unknown printshop. To solve the problem, we first sourced high-resolution scans of all of the Fifth Folio sheets from the Folger Shakespeare Library. Next, on the premise that Everingham, who was responsible for the deficiency of sheets and who was still at work in 1700, was the likeliest candidate, we ran the Folger scans through our machine learning pipeline, comparing distinctive types in the Fifth with those in the second section of the Fourth. The results were persuasive and conclusive: our comparison returned several matches, including a distinctively fractured *C*, a *W* with a markedly withered and recurved right arm (fourth diagonal), and a *K* with a miniscule fragment of type metal inked and evident between its two legs (fig. 6.15). The printers of the second section of the Fourth and the seventeen sheets in the Fifth were one and the same: Robert Everingham.

The sequence of events that led to Everingham's reprinting the deficient sheets are unknown and likely unknowable, yet it remains a fascinating subject for speculation. Did Wellington confront Everingham and threaten to raise the issue with The Stationers' Company, jeopardizing Everingham's reputation? Wellington's motive may have been more mundane: Everingham was the natural candidate to reprint his own work, and perhaps such lapses occurred regularly enough to excuse the printer's oversight. Regardless, Everingham evidently made good on the original contract, supplying the deficient sheets to be bound with belatedly sold copies of the Fourth Folio—though not without introducing additional flaws: the reprinted sheets, for instance, lack the borders that frame the text in the originals (fig. 1.8).

CODA: IMPLICATIONS

Unmasking the Fourth Folio's nameless printers adds little to our knowledge of Shakespeare's text. As Bowers noted in 1951, the Folio possesses no independent authority—for one thing, Shakespeare had been dead for seven decades at the time of its publication—and so revealing the individuals responsible for its printing would amount only to filling "a small gap in the information we should like to have" (Bowers 1951, 241). But if the substance of our findings is slight, our method offers a weighty lesson about the future drift of analytical bibliography. More precisely, our algorithmic analysis of the Fourth Folio's types demonstrates the promise of computation as an ameliorative tool in the bibliographer's toolkit. And new tools are needed. According to one recent analysis, sixty-four percent of editions listed in the ESTC are unattributed (Tolonen et al. 2021). Plenty of sleuthing remains to be done. And as more evidence is made available in digital forms of media, a new bibliographical practice lies in the direction of interdisciplinarity and automation.

APPENDIX: DAMAGED CHARACTER LOCATIONS

Abbreviations
FH—A Fond Husband (Everingham, 1685; ESTC R15791)
CG—Court of the Gentiles, Part 4 (Macock, 1677; ESTC R25438)
CG3—Court of the Gentiles, Part 4, Book 3 ([Macock] for John Hill, 1678; ESTC R16919)
MM—Man of Mode (Macock, 1684; ESTC R25438)
F5—Fifth Folio (Folger Shakespeare Library, Call no. S2915 Fo.4 nos.28, 33)
F4—Fourth Folio (ESTC R25621)

Locations of damaged characters in Figure 6.14
Row 1: "E" / F4 / sig. Bb1r, page 1, col. 1, line 1; "E" / F4 / sig. *Ddd6r, page 311, col. 1, line 36; "E" / FH / sig. D2v, page 22, line 23;

Row 2: "W" / F4 / sig. Bb1r, page 1, col. 2, line 5; "W" / F4 / sig. Xx4v, page 236, col. 2, line 37; "W" / FH / sig. F4r, page 41, line 40;

Row 3: "T" / F4 / sig. Bb1r, page 1, col. 1, line 14; "T" / F4 / sig. Tt4v, page 212, col. 2, line 26; "T" / FH / sig. H1r, page [51], line 7;

Row 4: "B" / F4 /sig. Bb1r, page 1, col. 2 line 32; "B" / F4 /sig. Ss2v, page 196, col. 1, line 34; "B" / FH / sig. H2v, page 54, line 15;

Row 5: "W" / F4 /sig. Bb1r, page 1, col. 2, line 5; "W" / F4 / sig. Nn1v, page 134, col. 1, line 50; "W" / FH / sig. B3r, page 7, line 21;

Row 6: "N" / F4 / sig. Bb1r, page 1, col. 2, line 23; "N" / F4 / sig. Cc6v, page 24, col. 1, line 17; "N" / FH / sig. H2r, page 53, line 3;

Row 7: "M" / F4 / sig. Bb1r, page 1, col. 2, line 16; "M" / F4 / sig. Zz5v, page 262, col. 2, line 49; "M" / FH / sig. G3v, page 48, line 9;

Row 8: "A" / F4 / sig. Bb1r, page 1, col. 2, line 26; "A" / F4 / sig. Ff6r, page 59, col. 2, line 54; "A" / FH / sig. H3r, page 55, line 14;

Row 9: "G" / F4 / sig. Bb1r, page 1, col. 2, line 7; "G" / F4 / sig. Rr1r, page 181, col. 1, line 25; "G" / FH / sig. G3r, page 49, line 1;

Row 10: "M" / F4 / sig. Bb1r, page 1, col. 1, line 7; "M" / F4 / sig. Aaa2r, page 267, col. 1, line 1; "M" / FH / sig. C3r, page 15, line 22;

Row 11: "B" / F4 / sig. Bb1r, page 1, col. 2, line 32; "B" / F4 / sig. Dd3r, page 29, col. 2, line 56; "B" / FH / sig. H3r, page 55, line 30;

Row 12: "R" / F4 / sig. Bb1r, page 1, col. 1, line 19; "R" / F4 / sig. Xx2r, page 231, col. 1, line 27; "R" / FH / sig. D2v, page 22, line 20

Locations of damaged characters in Figure 6.16

Row 1: "W" / F4 / sig. Eee6r, page 59, col. 2, line 1; "W" / F4 / sig. Lll3v, page 126, col. 1, line 17; "W" / CG3 / sig. E3r, page 37, line 16;

Row 2: "M" / F4 / sig. Eee6r, page 59, col. 2, line 14; "M" / F4 / sig. Qqq5v, page 190, col. 1, line 37; "M" / CG / sig. K2r, page 75, line 40;

Row 3: "N" / F4 / sig. Eee6r, page 59, col. 1, line 3; "N" / F4 / sig. Fff3v, page 66, col. 1, line 61; "N" / MM / sig. B1r, page 3, line 26;

Row 4: "L" / F4 / sig. Eee6r, page 59, col. 1, line 19; "L" / F4 / sig. Lll4r, page 127, col. 2, line 44; "L" / CG3 / sig. X1v, page 156, line 8;

Row 5: "C" / F4 / sig. Eee6r, page 59, col. 1, line 1; "C" / F4 / sig. Hhh4v, page 92, col. 2, line 54; "C" / MM / sig. F4r, page 41, line 29;

Row 6: "A" / F4 / sig. Eee6r, page 59, col. 1, line 35; "A" / F4 / sig. Kkk5v, page 118, col. 1, line 32; "A" / CG / sig. Y3v, page 174, line 36;

Row 7: "W" / F4 / sig. Eee6r, page 59, col. 2, line 1; "W" / F4 / sig. Fff6v, page 72, col. 1, line 16; "W" / CG / sig. Rr2v, page 316, line 24;

Row 8: "T" / F4 / sig. Eee6r, page 59, col. 1, line 35; "T" / F4 / sig. Iii5r, page 105, col. 1, line 18; "T" / MM / sig. D3r, page 23, line 26;

Row 9: "K" / F4 / sig. Eee6r, page 59, col. 2, line 32; "K" / F4 / sig. Mmm1v, page 134, col. 1, line 3; "K" / CG3 / sig. L4r, page 79, line 25

Locations of damaged characters in Figure 6.20

Row 1: "K" / F4 / sig. Bb1r, page 1, col. 1, line 5; "K" / F4 / sig. Ii4v, page 92, col. 2, line 18; "K" / F5, sig. *Ccc5v, page 298, col. 2, line 43;

Row 2: "C" / F4 / sig. Bb1r, page 1, col. 1, line 24; "C" / F4 / sig. Bb6r, page 11, col. 1, line 14; "C" / F5 / sig. Ii4r, page 91, col. 1, line 57;

Row 3: "B" / F4 / sig. Bb1r, page 1, col. 2, line 8; "B" / F4 / sig. Gg1r, page 61, col. 1, line 25; "B" / F5 / sig. *Ccc4v, page 296, col. 1, line 39;

Row 4: "W" / F4 / sig. Bb1r, page 1, col. 1, line 23; "W" / F4 / sig. Gg2v, page 64, col. 2, line 11; "W" / F5 / sig. Xx5v, page 238, col. 2, line 66

Row 5: "W" / F4 / sig. Bb1r, page 1, col. 1, line 36; "W" / F4 / sig. Bb3v, page 6, col. 2, line 4; "W" / F5 / sig. Bb4v, page 8, col. 2, line 44

REFERENCE LIST

Albany Centinel. 1805. Untitled article. July 23, 1805. Page 3, column 1.

"Alice Brownlow or Brownlowe or Sherard 1659–1721." In Book Owners Online, edited by David Pearson. Accessed December 7, 2022. https://www.bookowners.online/Alice_Brownlow_1659–1721.

Anonymous. 1661. *Tom Tyler and His Wife: An Excellent Old Play*. ESTC R1948.

August, Hannah. 2022. *Playbooks and Their Readers in Early Modern England*. New York: Routledge.

Baldwin, T. W. 1957. *Shakspere's Love's Labor's Won: New Evidence from the Account Books of an Elizabethan Bookseller*. Carbondale: Southern Illinois University Press.

Bartlett, Henrietta C. 1939. *A Census of Shakespeare's Plays in Quarto, 1594–1709*. Revised edition. New Haven: Yale University Press.

Bartlett, Henrietta C., and Alfred W. Pollard. 1916. *A Census of Shakespeare's Plays in Quarto, 1594–1709*. New Haven: Yale University Press.

Beaumont, Francis, and John Fletcher. 1647. *Comedies and Tragedies. Written by Francis Beaumont and John Fletcher, Gentlemen*. ESTC R22900.

Beaumont, Francis, and John Fletcher. 1679. *Fifty Comedies and Tragedies. Written by Francis Beaumont and John Fletcher, Gentlemen*. ESTC R13766.

Belanger, Terry. 1975. "Tonson, Wellington and the Shakespeare Copyrights." In *Studies in the Book Trade in Honour of Graham Pollard*, edited by Michael Turner, 195–209. Oxford: Oxford Bibliographical Society.

Benjamin, Walter. 1968. "Theses on the Philosophy of History." In *Illuminations*, edited by Hannah Arendt, translated by Harry Zohn, 253–64. New York: Schocken Books.

Bidwell, John. 2002. "French Paper in English Books." In *The Cambridge History of the Book in Britain, Volume 4: 1557–1695*, edited by John Barnard and D. F. McKenzie with Maureen Bell, 583–601. Cambridge: Cambridge University Press.

Black, N. W., and Matthias Shaaber. 1937. *Shakespeare's Seventeenth-Century Editors, 1632–1685*. New York: MLA.

Bland, Mark. 2010. *A Guide to Early Printed Books and Manuscripts*. London: Wiley.

Blayney, Peter W. M. 1973. "The Prevalence of Shared Printing In the Early Seventeenth Century." *The Papers of the Bibliographical Society of America* 67, no. 4: 437–63.

———. 1982. *The Texts of King Lear and Their Origins*. Cambridge: Cambridge University Press.

———. 1990. *The Bookshops in Paul's Cross Churchyard*. London: Bibliographical Society.

———. 1991. *The First Folio of Shakespeare*. Washington, DC: The Folger Shakespeare Library.

Boulton, Jeremy. 1996. "Wage Labour in Seventeenth-Century London." *Economic History Review* 49, no. 2: 268–90.

Bourne, Claire M. L. 2020. *Typographies of Performance in Early Modern England*. Oxford: Oxford University Press.

Bourne, Claire M. L., and Jason Scott-Warren. 2022. "'thy unvalued Booke': John Milton's Copy of the Shakespeare First Folio." *Milton Quarterly* 56: 1–85.

Bowers, Fredson. 1951. "Robert Roberts: A Printer of Shakespeare's Fourth Folio." *Shakespeare Quarterly* 2, no. 3: 241–46.

"A Catalogue of some Plays Printed for R. Bentley." 1691. In *Madam Fickle: or, The Witty False Ones*, by Thomas D'Ursey. ESTC R31389.

Connor, Francis X. 2014. *Literary Folios and Ideas of the Book in Early Modern England*. New York: Palgrave-Macmillan.

Cordell, Ryan. 2020. "Speculative Bibliography." *Anglia* 138, no. 3: 519–31. https://doi.org/10.1515/ang-2020-0041.

Craig, Heidi. 2020. "English Rag-Women and Early Modern Paper Production." In *Women's Labour and the History of the Book in Early Modern England*, edited by Valerie Wayne, 29–46. London: The Arden Shakespeare.

Craig, Hugh, and Arthur F. Kinney, eds. 2009. *Shakespeare, Computers, and the Mystery of Authorship*. Cambridge: Cambridge University Press.

Dawson, Giles E. 1952. "Some Bibliographical Irregularities in the Shakespeare Fourth Folio." *Studies in Bibliography* 4: 93–103.

Depledge, Emma. 2018. *Shakespeare's Rise to Cultural Prominence: Politics, Print and Alteration, 1642–1700*. Cambridge: Cambridge University Press.

Donovan, Kevin J. 1991. "Jonson's Texts in the First Folio." In *Ben Jonson's 1616 Folio*, edited by Jennifer Brady and W. H. Herendeen, 23–37. Newark: University of Delaware Press.

Dugas, Don-John. 2002. "Philip Chetwind and the Shakespeare Third Folio." *Harvard Library Bulletin* 14, no. 1: 29–46.

Erne, Lukas. 2023. "The Two Gentlemen of Zurich: Marcus Stapfer and Johann Rudolph Hess, Swiss Travellers to England (1611–13), and Their Shakespeare Quartos." *The Library* 24, no. 1: 51–67.

Estill, Laura. 2015. *Dramatic Extracts in Seventeenth-Century English Manuscripts: Watching, Reading, Changing Plays*. Newark, DE: University of Delaware Press.

Farmer, Alan B. 2016. "Playbooks and the Question of Ephemerality." In *The Book in History, The Book as History: New Intersections of the Material Text: Essays in Honor of David Scott Kastan*, edited by Heidi Brayman, Jesse M. Lander, and Zachary Lesser, 87–125. New Haven: Yale University Press.

Foxon, D. F. 1956. "Another Skeleton in Thomas J. Wise's Cupboard." *Times Literary Supplement*, October 19, 1956.

Galbraith, Steven K. 2010. "English Literary Folios 1593–1623: Studying Shifts in Format." In *Tudor Books and Readers: Materiality and the Construction of Meaning*, edited by John N. King, 46–67. Cambridge: Cambridge University Press.

Gants, David L, and Tom Lockwood. n.d. "The Printing and Publishing of Ben Jonson's Works." The Cambridge Edition of the Works of Ben Jonson Online. Accessed December 7, 2022. https://universitypublishingonline.org/cambridge/benjonson/k/essays/printing_publishing_essay/.

Garlick, Karen. 1986. "A Brief Review of the History of Sizing and Resizing Practices." *The Book and Paper Group Annual* 5: n.p.

Gaskell, Philip. 1995. *A New Introduction to Bibliography*. New Castle: Oak Knoll Press.

Goyal, Kartik, Chris Dyer, Christopher Warren, Max G'Sell, and Taylor Berg-Kirkpatrick. 2020. "A Probabilistic Generative Model for Typographical Analysis of Early Modern Printing." *ArXiv:2005.01646v1 [cs.LG]*. http://arxiv.org/abs/2005.01646.

Greg, W. W. 1951. "The Rationale of Copy-Text." *Studies in Bibliography* 3: 19–36.

———. 1962. *A Bibliography of the English Printed Drama to the Restoration*. Vol. 3, *Collections, Appendix, Reference Lists*. London: The Bibliographical Society.

Hailey, Carter. 2011. "The Best Crowne Paper." In *Foliomania! Stories Behind Shakespeare's Most Important Book*, edited by Owen Williams with Caryn Lazzuri, 8–14. Washington, DC: The Folger Shakespeare Library.

Hansen, Lara. 2014. "Between the Sheets: The Use of Paper Evidence in Bibliographic Reconstruction of the Shakespeare First Folio." PhD dissertation. University of Nevada, Reno. Accessed December 1, 2023. https://scholarworks.unr.edu/bitstream/handle/11714/2901/Hansen_unr_0139D_11541.pdf?sequence=1&isAllowed=y.

Hansen, Lara, and Eric Rasmussen. 2017. "Shakespeare Without Rules: The Fifth Shakespeare Folio and Market Demand in the Early 1700s." In *Canonising Shakespeare: Stationers and the Book Trade, 1640–1740*, edited by Emma Depledge and Peter Kirwan, 38–54. Cambridge: Cambridge University Press.

Higgins, Ben. 2022. *Shakespeare's Syndicate: The First Folio, its Publishers, and the Early Modern Book Trade*. Oxford: Oxford University Press.

Hinman, Charlton. 1947. "Mechanized Collation: A Preliminary Report." *The Papers of the Bibliographical Society of America* 41, no. 2: 99–106.

———. 1955. "Mechanized Collation at the Houghton Library." *Harvard Library Bulletin* 9: 132–34.

———. 1963. *The Printing and Proof-Reading of the First Folio of Shakespeare*. Oxford: At the Clarendon Press.

Hirsh, James. 2002. "Act Divisions in the Shakespeare First Folio." *Papers of the Bibliographical Society of America* 96, no. 2: 219–56.

Hooks, Adam G. 2016. "Afterword: The Folio as Fetish." In *The Cambridge Companion to Shakespeare's First Folio*, edited by Emma Smith, 185–96. Cambridge: Cambridge University Press.

Hooks, Adam G., and Zachary Lesser, eds. n.d. *Shakespeare Census*. Accessed December 7, 2022. https://shakespearecensus.org.

Hubbard, Eleanor. 2015. "Reading, Writing, and Initialing: Female Literacy in Early Modern London." *Journal of British Studies* 54: 553–77.

Johns, Adrian. 2010. "Ink." In *Materials and Expertise in Early Modern Europe: Between Market and Laboratory*, edited by E.C. Spary and Ursula Klein, 101–24. Chicago: University of Chicago Press.

Jonson, Ben. 1616. *The Workes*. ESTC S126501.

———. 1633–1641. *The Workes*. Volumes 2–3. ESTC S428.

———. 1640. *The Workes*. Volume 1. ESTC S112456.

Jowett, John. 2011. "The Type of the Shakespeare First Folio." In *Foliomania! Stories Behind Shakespeare's Most Important Book*, edited by Owen Williams with Caryn Lazzuri, 15–20. Washington, DC: The Folger Shakespeare Library.

———. 2015. "Full Pricks and Great P's: Spellings, Punctuation, Accidentals." In *Shakespeare and Textual Studies*, edited by M. J. Kidnie and Sonia Massai, 317–31. Cambridge: Cambridge University Press.

Kirwan, Peter. 2015. *Shakespeare and the Idea of Apocrypha: Negotiating the Boundaries of the Dramatic Canon*. Cambridge: Cambridge University Press.

Knight, Jeffrey Todd. 2013. *Bound to Read: Compilations, Collections, and the Making of Renaissance Literature*. Philadelphia: University of Pennsylvania Press.

———. 2017. "Economies of Scale: Shakespeare and Book History: Shakespeare and Book History." *Literature Compass* 14, no. 6: n.p. https://doi.org/10.1111/lic3.12393.

Lesser, Zachary. 2011. "Playbooks." In *The Oxford History of Popular Print Culture. I: Cheap Print in Britain and Ireland to 1660*, edited by Joad Raymond, 520–34. Oxford: Oxford University Press.

———. 2015. *Hamlet After Q1: An Uncanny History of the Shakespearean Text*. Philadelphia: University of Pennsylvania Press.

———. 2021. *Ghosts, Holes, Rips and Scrapes: Shakespeare in 1619, Bibliography in the Longue Durée*. Philadelphia: University of Pennsylvania Press.

Lesser, Zachary, and Whitney Trettien. 2021. "Material / digital." In *Shakespeare / Text: Contemporary Readings in Textual Studies, Editing and Performance*, edited by Claire M. L. Bourne, 402–23. London: The Arden Shakespeare.

Lidster, Amy. 2022. *Publishing the History Play in the Time of Shakespeare: Stationers Shaping a Genre*. Cambridge: Cambridge University Press.

Lindenbaum, Sarah. 2018. "Written in the Margent: Frances Wolfreston Revealed." *The Collation* (blog). June 21, 2018. https://collation.folger.edu/2018/06/frances-wolfreston-revealed/.

Lyons, Tara L. 2012. "Serials, Spinoffs, and Histories: Selling Shakespeare Collections Before the First Folio." *Philological Quarterly* 91, no. 2: 185–220.

———. 2023. "Library Records and the Stationers of London: The Bodleian Daybook, 1613–1620." *Textual Cultures* 16 (2023): 142–207.

Maguire, Laurie. 1999. "The Craft of Printing (1600)." In *A Companion to Shakespeare*, edited by David Scott Kastan, 434–49. Oxford: Blackwell Publishers.

Mandelbrote, Giles. 1997. "Richard Bentley's Copies: The Ownership of Copyrights in the Late 17th Century." In *The Book Trade & Its Customers, 1450–1900: Historical Essays for Robin Myers*, edited by Arnold Hunt, Giles Mandelbrote, and Alison Shell, 55–94. New Castle: Oak Knoll Press.

Massai, Sonia. 2007. *Shakespeare and the Rise of the Editor*. Cambridge: Cambridge University Press.

Masten, Jeffrey. 2016. *Queer Philologies: Sex, Language, and Affect in Shakespeare's Time*. Philadelphia: University of Pennsylvania Press.

Mayer, Jean-Christophe. 2015. "The Saint-Omer First Folio: Perspectives on a New Shakespearean Discovery." *Cahiers Élisabéthains: A Journal of English Renaissance Studies* 87, no. 1: 7–20.

———. 2018. *Shakespeare's Early Readers: A Cultural History from 1590 to 1800*. Cambridge: Cambridge University Press.

McKerrow, R. B., ed. 1910. *A Dictionary of Printers and Booksellers in England, Scotland and Ireland, and of Foreign Printers of English Books, 1557–1640*. London: Bibliographical Society.

Milton, John. 1632. "An Epitaph on the admirable Dramaticke Poet, VV. Shakespeare." In *William Shakespeares Comedies, Histories, and Tragedies.* London: Richard Meighen et al.

Mowery, Frank. 2011. "The Bindings of the Folger's First Folios." In *Foliomania! Stories Behind Shakespeare's Most Important Book*, edited by Owen Williams with Caryn Lazzuri, 32–39. Washington, DC: The Folger Shakespeare Library.

Moxon, Joseph. 1683. *Mechanick Exercises: Or, the Doctrine of Handy-works. Applied to the Art of Printing.* London: Joseph Moxon.

Murphy, Andrew. 2021. *Shakespeare in Print: A History and Chronology of Shakespeare Publishing.* Cambridge: Cambridge University Press.

Pepys, Samuel. 1976. *The Diary of Samuel Pepys.* Vol. 9, *1668–1669*, edited by Robert Latham and William Matthews. London: Bell.

Plomer, Henry R. 1907. *A Dictionary of the Booksellers and Printers Who Were at Work in England, Scotland and Ireland from 1641 to 1667.* London: Bibliographical Society.

Pollard, A. W. 1909. *Shakespeare Folios and Quartos: A Study in the Bibliography of Shakespeare's Plays, 1594–1685.* London: Methuen and Company.

Pollard, Graham. 1941. "Notes on the Size of the Sheet," *The Library*, 4th ser., 22, nos. 2–3: 105–37.

Pratt, Aaron. 2015. "Stab-Stitching and the Status of Early English Playbooks as Literature." *The Library*, 7th series, 16, no. 3: 304–28.

———. 2019. "Perfect." In *Collated & Perfect*, by Kathryn James and Aaron Pratt, 25–45. New Haven: Beinecke Library.

Prosdocimi, Lavinia. 2021. "Un fondo appartenuto alla *natio Anglica*. Il *First Folio* e altri libri inglesi della Biblioteca universataria." In *Intellettuali e Uomini di Corte: Padova e lo spazio europeo fra Cinque e Seicento*, edited by Ester Pietrobon. Rome: Donzelli and Padova University Press.

Prynne, William. 1633. *Histrio-mastix.* London: Michael Sparke.

Rasmussen, Eric, and Anthony James West, with Donald L. Bailey, Mark Farnsworth, Lara Hansen, Trey Jansen, and Sarah Stewart, eds. 2012. *The Shakespeare First Folios: A Descriptive Catalogue.* Basingstoke: Palgrave Macmillan.

Salzman, Paul. 2021. "Part / Whole." In *Shakespeare / Text: Contemporary Readings in Textual Studies, Editing and Performance*, edited by Claire M. L. Bourne, 299–315. London: Arden Shakespeare.

Schlueter, June. 2007. "Martin Droeshout Redivivus: Reassessing the Folio Engraving of Shakespeare." *Shakespeare Survey* 60: 237–51.

Schuckman, Christiaan. 1991. "The Engraver of the First Folio Portrait of William Shakespeare." *Print Quarterly* 8: 40–43.

Shakespeare, William. 1623. *Mr. William Shakespeares Comedies, Histories, & Tragedies. Published According to the True Original Copies.* STC 22273.

———. 1632. *Mr. William Shakespears Comedies, Histories, and Tragedies. Published According to the True Original Copies.* STC 22274.

———. 1664. *Mr. William Shakespeare's Comedies, Histories, and Tragedies. Published According to the True Original Copies.* Wing S2914.

———. 1685. *Mr. William Shakespear's Comedies, Histories, and Tragedies. Published According to the True Original Copies.* Wing S2917.

Spenser, Edmund. 1611. *The Faerie Queen. . . . Collected into One Volume.* ESTC S123122.

———. 1617. *The Faerie Queen. . . . Collected into One Volume*. ESTC S122304.
Sharpe, Will. 2013. "Authorship and Attribution." In *RSC Shakespeare: William Shakespeare and Others, Collaborative Plays*, edited by Jonathan Bate and Eric Rasmussen with Jan Sewell and Will Sharpe. London: Red Globe Press.
Sherman, William H. 2009. *Used Books: Marking Readers in Renaissance England*. Philadelphia: University of Pennsylvania Press.
Smith, Emma. 2015. *The Making of Shakespeare's First Folio*. Oxford: Bodleian Libraries.
———. 2016a. *Shakespeare's First Folio: Four Centuries of an Iconic Book*. Oxford: Oxford University Press.
———. 2016b. "Vamped Till Ready." *Times Literary Supplement*, April 8, 2016. https://www.the-tls.co.uk/articles/vamped-till-ready/.
"Some Books Printed, and Sold by R. Bentley and S. Magnes, in Russel-Street in Covent-Garden." 1686. In *The Amours of Count Teckeli and the Lady Aurora Veronica de Serini*, by Jean de Préchac. ESTC R25592
Stern, Tiffany. 2009. *Documents of Performance in Early Modern England*. Cambridge: Cambridge University Press.
Stevenson, Allan H. 1951. "Watermarks Are Twins." *Studies in Bibliography* 4: 57–235.
Syme, Holger Schott. 2008. "Unediting the Margin: Jonson, Marston, and the Theatrical Page." *English Literary Renaissance* 38, no. 1: 142–71.
Tanselle, G. Thomas. 1989. "Reproductions and Scholarship." *Studies in Bibliography* 42: 25–54.
Taylor, Gary, John Jowett, Terri Bourus, and Gabriel Egan, eds. 2016. *New Oxford Shakespeare: Critical Reference Edition*. Oxford: Oxford University Press.
Tolonen, Mikko, Mark J. Hill, Ali Zeeshan Ijaz, Ville Vaara, and Leo Lahti. 2021. "Examining the Early Modern Canon: The English Short Title Catalogue and Large-Scale Patterns of Cultural Production." In *Data Visualization in Enlightenment Literature and Culture*, edited by Ileana Baird, 63–119. Cham: Palgrave Macmillan. https://doi.org/10.1007/978-3-030-54913-8_3.
Trettien, Whitney. 2021. *Cut / Copy / Paste: Fragments from the History of Bookwork*. Minneapolis: University of Minnesota Press.
University of Oxford, Wadham College. n.d. "Oxford and Colonialism." Accessed December 7, 2022. https://oxfordandcolonialism.web.ox.ac.uk/wadham-college.
Walker, Alice. 1953. *Textual Problems of the First Folio*. Cambridge: Cambridge University Press.
Warren, Christopher N., Avery Wiscomb, Pierce Williams, Samuel V. Lemley, and Max G'Sell. 2021. "Canst Thou Draw Out Leviathan with Computational Bibliography? New Angles on Printing Thomas Hobbes' 'Ornaments' Edition." *Eighteenth-Century Studies* 54, no. 4: 827–59.
Warren, Christopher N., Pierce Wiliams, Shruti Rijhwani, and Max G'Sell. 2020. "Damaged Type and Areopagitica's Clandestine Printers." *Milton Studies* 62, no. 1: 1–47.
Weiss, Adrian. 1990. "Font Analysis as a Bibliographical Method: The Elizabethan Play-Quarto Printers and Compositors." *Studies in Bibliography* 43: 95–164.
———. 1991. "Bibliographical Methods for Identifying Unknown Printers in Elizabethan/Jacobean Books." *Studies in Bibliography* 44: 183–228.

Wells, Stanley. 2013. "Folios, the Second, Third, and Fourth." In *An A-Z Guide to Shakespeare*. Oxford: Oxford University Press. https://www.oxfordreference.com/view/10.1093/acref/9780191740763.001.0001/acref-9780191740763-e-227.

Werner, Sarah. 2016. "Digital First Folios." In *The Cambridge Companion to Shakespeare's First Folio*, edited by Emma Smith, 170–84. Cambridge: Cambridge University Press.

Williams, William P. 1977. "Chetwin, Crooke, and the Jonson Folios." *Studies in Bibliography* 30: 75–95.

Willoughby, E. E. 1932. *The Printing of the First Folio of Shakespeare*. Oxford: Bibliographical Society.

Wilson, John Dover, ed. 1955. William Shakespeare, *Romeo and Juliet*. Cambridge: Cambridge University Press.

CONTRIBUTORS

Taylor Berg-Kirkpatrick is Associate Professor in the Computer Science and Engineering Department at the University of California San Diego. His lab's research focuses on using machine learning to understand structured human data, including language, but also sources like music, document images, and other complex artifacts.

Erin C. Blake is the Senior Cataloger responsible for art and manuscripts at the Folger Shakespeare Library in Washington, DC. She is also a faculty member of Rare Book School at the University of Virginia, where she teaches "The History of Printed Book Illustration in the West." She holds a PhD in art history from Stanford University, and has written and lectured widely on issues related to book illustration.

Claire M. L. Bourne is Associate Professor of English at The Pennsylvania State University, where she teaches and writes about early modern literature, book history, and textual editing. She is author of *Typographies of Performance in Early Modern England* (2020) and coauthor of "'thy unvalued Booke': John Milton's Copy of the Shakespeare First Folio" (2022). She is currently editing *Henry the Sixth, Part 1*, for The Arden Shakespeare (Fourth Series).

Laura S. DeLuca is a PhD student at Carnegie Mellon University in the English Department. Her research interests include early modern drama and history, gender and sexuality studies, classical reception, and digital humanities.

Elizabeth Dieterich is a PhD Candidate in Literary and Cultural Studies at Carnegie Mellon University. Her research focuses on affective experiences of playgoing in early modernity, theatrical material culture, and Shakespeare in performance.

Kartik Goyal is Assistant Professor in the College of Computing at Georgia Tech. His research interests focus on developing probabilistic models of latent structure in naturally occurring data with applications in natural language processing and digital humanities.

Max G'Sell is a researcher at PDT Partners. Max was previously Associate Professor of Statistics at Carnegie Mellon University, where his research focused on adapting predictive models to guide or support scientific inference and inquiry, and on developing theory and methodology for data-guided hypothesis testing.

Samuel V. Lemley is Curator of Special Collections at Carnegie Mellon University Libraries. His work has appeared in *Papers of the Bibliographical Society of America (PBSA), The Library, Studies in Bibliography, Eighteenth-Century Studies,* and other journals.

Zachary Lesser is the Edward W. Kane Professor of English at the University of Pennsylvania. A general editor of The Arden Shakespeare (Fourth Series), for which he is editing *Macbeth*, Lesser is the author of *Ghosts, Holes, Rips and Scrapes: Shakespeare in 1619, Bibliography in the Longue Durée* (2021), *Hamlet After Q1: An Uncanny History of the Shakespearean Text* (2015), and *Renaissance Drama and the Politics of Publication: Readings in the English Book Trade* (2004). He is the cocreator of two online resources for the study of early printed drama: DEEP: Database of Early English Playbooks (with Alan B. Farmer) and the *Shakespeare Census* (with Adam Hooks).

Tara L. Lyons is Associate Professor of English at Illinois State University. Her scholarship on book history and early modern literature has been published in *PBSA, ELR, Philological Quarterly, Textual Cultures,* and within a number of edited collections, such as *The Cambridge Companion to Shakespeare's First Folio*. She has received grants from the Huntington, Folger, and Bodleian Libraries as well as from the Bibliographical Society of America.

Andrew Murphy is a Member of the Royal Irish Academy and a Fellow of Trinity College Dublin, where he is 1867 Professor of English Literature. His major publications include *Shakespeare in Print: A History and Chronology of Shakespeare Publishing* (second edition, 2021), *Ireland, Reading and Cultural Nationalism: Bringing the Nation to Book* (2018), and *Shakespeare for the People: Working-Class Readers 1800–1900* (2008).

D. J. Schuldt has a PhD in English from Carnegie Mellon University and is currently working on a master's degree in library and information science at Simmons University. His interests focus on rare book librarianship and historical archives.

Kari Thomas is an advanced PhD student at Carnegie Mellon University in the History Department. Her work focuses on digital humanities and how social media and other digital networks influence collective historical memory and commemoration. Her love of rare books comes from many hours spent in the Wiktenauer digital repository trying to make sense of fifteenth-century German *fectbuchen*.

Nikolai Vogler is a PhD student at University of California, San Diego in the Computer Science and Engineering Department, where he researches natural language processing and machine learning for historical documents and the digital humanities.

Christopher N. Warren is Professor of English with a courtesy appointment in History at Carnegie Mellon University. He is Principal Investigator of the NEH-funded digital humanities project "Freedom and the Press before Freedom of the Press" and co-founder of Six Degrees of Francis Bacon.

Keith Webster is Helen and Henry Posner, Jr. Dean of the University Libraries at Carnegie Mellon University.

INDEX

Note: Italicized page references indicate illustrations.

Aitken, George, 114
Allott, Mary, 23–26
Allott, Robert, 20–21, *22*, 23, 26
All's Well That Ends Well (Shakespeare), *104*
anagrams, 108
Antony and Cleopatra (Shakespeare), 20, 23
Aspley, William, 17, 20, 23
Astor family, 101
Astor Library, 115
author portraits
    Droeshout portrait, four states of, 65, *66*, 67, 69–70, *70*, 72
    Droeshout portrait, location of, *73*, *74*, 74–75
    standard location of, *61*, 61–62
authorship, shifting conceptions of, 105
Avezac, Louise d', 114

Bagford, John, 99
Bartholomew Fair (Jonson), 21
Barton, Thomas Pennant, 101, 112, 114
Bassett, Thomas, 92
Bayly, Lewis, *The Practice of Piety*, 21, 26, 28
Beaumont, Francis, 28, 58
    Fifty Comedies and Tragedies (with Fletcher), 91–93, 138
    Scornful Lady, The (with Fletcher), 128, *129*
Bedford, Francis, 111
Benjamin, Walter, 116
Bennet, Joseph, 126
Bentley, Richard, 89–90, 91–92, *92*, 125, 131, 139
Berlin State Library, 102
bibliographical analysis. *See* computational bibliography
Bibliothèque National de France (BnF), 102
Bill, John, 83
bindings, 10, 79, 100, 110–11
Black Bear shop, 16, 20–21, 26
Blayney, Peter W. M., 53–55, 119, 121, 130
Blount, Edward, 16–17, 20
Bodleian Library, Oxford University, 75, 104–5
Bodmer Foundation, Geneva, 102, 110
Boston Public Library, 101, 108

Bourne, Claire M.L., 106
Bourne, Elizabeth, 110
Bowers, Fredson, 2, 119, 121, 126, 128–30, 135–36, 142
Brewster, Edward, 29, 92, 125, 131
British Library, 108, 113
British Museum, 113, 114
Brownlowe, Alice, 7–8, *8*, 107, *109*
Brownlowe, Alice (Alicia), 8, *8*, 107, *109*
Brownlowe, John, 8
Brownlowe, Margaret, 8, *8*, *9*, 107, *109*
Buffalo and Erie County Public Library, 101, 115
Burge, William, 115

Calhoun, John, 115
California State Library, Sutro, 101
Carnegie Mellon University (CMU) Libraries
    Hinman Collator, 5, 123, *124*
    Inventing Shakespeare: Text, Technology, and the Four Folios (exhibition), 4, 5
    From Stage to Page: 400 Years of Shakespeare in Print (exhibition), 4–5
casting-off process, 55
censorship, 103, *104*
Cervantes, 16
Charlewood, John, 38
Charnock, Stephen, *Works*, 129
Chaucer, Geoffrey, 80
Chetwinde, Philip, 23–28, 74, 88
Child, Mary, 108–10
Chiswell, Richard, 29, 92, 125, 131
Clark, Mary, 126, 128
Clifton, Charles, 101, 115
Clothworkers' Company, 23
Colgate University, 108
Colin Clout (Spenser), 84
collation technology, 5, 123, *124*
Collinges, John, *The History of Conformity*, 129
colonialism and slavery legacies, 114–16
Comedy of Errors, The (Shakespeare), 19
commonplacing, 106, *107*
composite and facsimile copies, 111–14, *112*, *113*

compositors, 38, 95
    See also typography
computational bibliography
    collation technology and, 123, *124*
    damaged type and, *120*, 120–21
    Fifth Folio printer as Everingham, 139–42, *140*, *141*
    methodology, 121–25, *122*
    printer one as Roberts, 128–33, *129*, *131*, *132*, *133*
    printer two as Everingham, *134*, 135
    printer three as Macock, 133, 135–38, *137*, *138*, *139*
Condell, Henry, 2, 11, 18, 20, 61, 72
Connor, Francis X., 2
Constable, Henry, "The Shepherd's Song of Venus and Adonis," 108
Conyers, George, 92
Copinger, Elizabeth, 108
copyright. *See* rights-holders
Cordell, Ryan, 123
Cotes, Ellen, 26
Cotes, Richard, 21, 23, 26
Cotes, Thomas, 21, 23
Court of the Gentiles, The (Gale), 136, *137*
Cowper, Dorothy, 110
Craig, Heidi, 36
cultural authority, 79–80

damaged types, 56–58, 120–21
    See also computational bibliography
Daniel, Samuel, 16, 80
Darby, John, 126
Dawson, Giles, 7, 139
Day, John, 38
deaccessions, 75, 105
decoration and ornamentation, 23, *24*, *25*, 45, 46, *47*, 49, 50, 63, 128–30, *129*, 135
Depledge, Emma, 4
Description of the King's Royal Palace and Gardens at Loo, A (Harris), 128, 130
design
    indents, 51
    of final pages of playtexts, 29, *29*, *47*, 49–50
    of first pages of playtexts, *30*, 45, 46–48
    margins, 46, *48*, 82
    of opening spread, 42–44, *43* (*see also* title pages)
    ornamentation and decoration, 23, *24*, *25*, 45, 46, *47*, 49, 50, 63, 128–30, *129*, 135
    of prefatory pages, 44, 44–45
    rule lines, 31, 45–46
    textual divisions, 49, 51–52

of typical pages of playtexts, *46*, 49, *81*, 82
    See also typography
digital facsimiles, value of, 122–23
    See also computational bibliography
dramatis personae lists, 19, 20, 50
Droeshout, Martin
    identity, 67–68
    James Marquis of Hamilton portrait, 70–71
    The Prophecies of the Twelve Sybills engraving, 71, *71*
    Shakespeare portrait, four states of, 65, *66*, 67, 69–70, *70*, 72
    Shakespeare portrait, location of, *73*, 74, 74–75
    Spiritual Warfare engraving, 68
Dryden, John
    Evening's Love, 28
    Marriage à la Mode, 114
D'Urfey, Thomas, *A Fond Husband*, *134*, 135

East India Company, 115
"editions" *vs.* "states," 68–69
editorial process. *See* printing and publishing process
editorial theory, 105
EEBO (Early English Books Online), 127, 138
Endymion (Lyly), 38
Englands Helicon, 108
errors
    in illustration printing, 67
    textual, 7, 23, 26, 30, 53–55, *54*, 117, *118*
ESTC (English Short Title Catalogue), 125, 126, 129, 142
Etherege, George, 28
    Man of Mode, or, Sr Fopling Flutter, The, 136, *137*
Evening's Love (Dryden), 28
Everingham, Robert, 119, 126, 128, 135, 141–42

facsimile and composite copies, 111–14, *112*, *113*
Faerie Queene, The (Spenser), 84
Fase, Niccolas, 110
Field, Richard, 13
"Fifth" Folio, 7, *30*, 31, 139–42, *140*
Fifty Comedies and Tragedies (Beaumont and Fletcher), 91–93, 138
First Folio. *See* Folio, First
Flesher, Miles, 138
Fletcher, John, 28, 58
    Fifty Comedies and Tragedies (with Beaumont), 91–93, 138
    Scornful Lady, The (with Beaumont), 128, *129*

Florio, John, 16
Folger, Henry, 101, 105
Folger Shakespeare Library, 101, 110, 115
Folio, First
    copies, number of surviving, 97 (*see also* provenance)
    design (*see* design; title pages, Four Folios)
    marketing strategies, 82–84, 86
    prominence of, 2–4
    publication process, 15, 16–18, 20, 79, 80–82
    vs. 1619 quartos, 15–16, 18–19, 38, 85–86
    text categorization and systematization, 19–20
Folio, Second
    copies, number of surviving, 4, 97 (*see also* provenance)
    imprint, 21, *22*, 74
    marketing strategies, 87
    Milton's poem in, 3, 33, 87
    and prominence of First Folio, 2–4
    publication process, 20–23
Folio, Third
    copies, number of surviving, 4, 89, 97–98 (*see also* provenance)
    imprint, 26, *27*, 74
    marketing strategies, 87–88
    and prominence of First Folio, 2–4
    publication process, 23–28
    second issue of (1664), 5, *6*, 28, 74–75, 87–88, 89, 93, 97–98
Folio, Fourth
    copies, number of surviving, 4, 97 (*see also* provenance)
    imprint, 119, 131, *132*, 138, *140*
    marketing strategies, 89–91, *90*, 92, *92*
    printer identification (*see* computational bibliography)
    and prominence of First Folio, 2–4
    publication process, *29*, 29–31, 88, 117–19
    reprinting of ("Fifth" Folio), 7, *30*, 31, 139–42, *140*
Folio, "Fifth," 7, *30*, 31, 139–42, *140*
folio, as term, 1–2, 34, 79
folio format
    prestige of, 17–18, 80
    vs. quarto format, 15–16, 79, 81, 83–84
    structure of, 34, *35*, 52–53, 79
    as "supersized," 78–79, 88, *89*
Fond Husband, A (D'Urfey), *134*, 135
font analysis, 120, 123
    See also computational bibliography
fonts. *See* typography

Fourth Folio. *See* Folio, Fourth
Free Library of Philadelphia, 101, 106
Frick Art Museum, Pittsburgh, *From Stage to Page: 400 Years of Shakespeare in Print* (exhibition), 4–5
Fuller, "Mad Jack," 115
Furness, Horace Howard, 111

Gain, John, 126
Galbraith, Steven, 35, 81
Gale, Theophilus, *The Court of the Gentiles*, 136, *137*
Gallathea (Lyly), 38
Gaskell, Philip, 40, 125, 126
gendered ordering of characters, 19, 20
generic categorization, 19, 43, 82
Greg, W. W., 56, 118, 122
Grenville, Richard, 115

Halliwell-Phillipps, James Orchard, 111
Hamilton, James Marquis of, 70–71
Hamlet (Shakespeare), 7, 14, 17, 30, 38, 98, 99, 102, 106, 117, *118*
Hansen, Laura, 139
Harington, John, 85
Harris, John, 113
Harris, Walter, *A Description of the King's Royal Palace and Gardens at Loo*, 128, 130
Harvard University, 101
Hawkins, Richard, 21, 23
Heminges, John, 2, 11, 18, 20, 61, 72
1 Henry IV (Shakespeare), 99
2 Henry IV (Shakespeare), 102
Henry V (Shakespeare), 15, 20, 23, 85, 98
1 Henry VI (Shakespeare), 14, 29
2 Henry VI (Shakespeare), 14, 15, 17, 23, 29, 85, 98
3 Henry VI (Shakespeare), 14, 15, 85, 98, 99
Herbert, William, 20, 23
Herringman, Henry, 28–29, 92, 93, 125, 131
Hibbert, George, 115
Hills, Henry, Jr., 126, 138
Hinman, Charlton, 5, 56, 58, 121, 123–24
History of Conformity, The (Collinges), 129
History of Thomas Lord Cromwell, The (attributed to Shakespeare), 26, 28, 87–88
Histrio-mastix: The Players Scourge (Prynne), 77, 79–80, 93–94
Hodkins, Thomas, 126
Hooks, Adam, 3, 4, 96
Huntington, Henry, 101, 111

indents, 51
intaglio printing technique, 62, 64–65, *65*, 67
Ives, Brayton, 101

Jaggard, Isaac, 2, 16–17, 20, 21, 34, 37–38
Jaggard, William, 15–16, 20, 34, 36–38, 85
James, King of England, *Works*, *61*, 62, *65*
Johnson, Samuel, 3
Johnstoune, William, 106
Jonson, Ben, 16, 28, 79, 108
    Bartholomew Fair, 21
    poem in Four Folios, 17–18, 42, 72–74
    Works (1616), 37, *60*, 60–61, *65*, 80, 81, 82, *83*
    Works (1640-1641), 93
    Works (1692), 92, 93
Julius Caesar (Shakespeare), 2, 98

Kemble, John Philip, 110–11
King, Martha, 110
King Lear (Shakespeare), 15, 85, 98, 108
King's Men, 16, 18
Kirkman, Francis, 28
Kirwan, Peter, 4
Knight, Jeffrey Todd, 2, 84, 122–23
Knight, Joseph, 125, 131, 133, 138

Laoutaris, Chris, 3
Lenox, James, 101
Lesser, Zachary, 122
Lindenbaum, Sarah, 108
Livingston, Cora, 101, 114
Livingston, Philip, 114
Livingston, Robert, 114
London Prodigal, The (attributed to Shakespeare), 26, 28, 87
Lord Chamberlain's Men, 17
Love's Labour's Lost (Shakespeare), 1, 17, 19, 23
Love's Labour's Won (Shakespeare), 100
Lyly, John
    Endymion, 38
    Gallathea, 38
Lyons, Tara L., 19

Macbeth (Shakespeare), 2, 102, *103*
machine learning technology. *See* computational bibliography
Macock, John, 119, 126, 128, 133, 135–38
Magnes, James, 89–90, 91
Maguire, Lauri, 55–56
Maid of Honour, The (Massinger), 21
Man of Mode, or, Sr Fopling Flutter, The, (Etheredge) 136, *137*

Marjoribanks, Dudley Coutts, 115
marketing strategies
    for Beaumont and Fletcher folio, 91–93
    for First Folio, 82–84, 86
    for Second Folio, 87
    for Third Folio, 87–88
    for Fourth Folio, 89–91, *90*, 92, *92*
Marlowe, Christopher, 16
Marriage à la Mode (Dryden), 114
Marriot, Richard, 92
Martyn, John, 92
Massai, Sonia, 4
Massinger, Philip
    Maid of Honour, The, 21
    Roman Actor, The, 21
Maxwell, Anne, 128–30
Measure for Measure (Shakespeare), 102
Meighen, Richard, 21, 23
Meisei University, 102, 106
Merchant of Venice, The (Shakespeare), 15, 38, 85, 98, 108
Merry Wives of Windsor, The (Shakespeare), 15, 21, *78*, 79, 85, 98
Middleton, Thomas, 28
    World Tost at Tennis, The (with Rowley), *63*, 64
Midsummer Night's Dream, A (Shakespeare), 15, 85, 98
Millington, Thomas, 14, 16
Mills College, 97, 115
Milton, John, 3, 33, *48*, 87, 106
Montaigne, 16
Morgan, J. P., 101
Mount Stuart library, 103–4
Moxon, Joseph, 33
Mr. William Shakespeares Comedies, Histories, and Tragedies. See *entries at* Folio
Much Ado About Nothing (Shakespeare), 17, 23, 24, *25*, 102
Munro, Thomas, 115

Newcomb, Thomas, Jr., 126
New York Public Library, 101, 115
Noble Kinsmen (Shakespeare), 98

Okell, Elizabeth, 111
Oldcastle (Shakespeare), 85
ornamentation and decoration, 23, *24*, *25*, 45, 46, *47*, 49, 50, 63, 128–30, *129*, 135
Othello (Shakespeare), 19, 21, 30, 98, 102, 108, *109*
Oudin, Cæsar, 16
Oxford University, 75, 101, 104–5

Panizzi, Anthony, 113
paper
    sizes of: crown, 34–35, 36, 77, 79, 82; demy, 88, 93; pot, 82
    supply of, 16, 34–37, 77, 80–81, 82, 88, 93
Passe, Simon de, 67
Pavier, Thomas, 15, 16, 38, 85
Pepys, Samuel, 28
Pericles (Shakespeare), 14, 15, 26, 28, 75, 85, 87, 88, 98, 102, 138
Petworth House, 110
pilcrows, 51
Plomer, Henry R., 136
Poems (Shakespeare), 98, 102
Pollard, A. W., 38
Ponsonby, William, 16
Poole, William, *Annotations Upon the Holy Bible*, 130–32, *131*, *133*
Practice of Piety, The (Bayly), 21, 26, 28
Pratt, Aaron, 114
Princeton University, 101
printing and publishing process
    binding process, 10, 79, 100
    collaborative networks, 16–17, 21, 26, 29, 92, 117–19, 125, 128–29
    collected works of other playwrights, *60*, 60–61, 80, 91–93
    costs of production, 16, 34, 35, 72, 80–82, 93
    editorial theory and, 105
    of individual playtexts by Shakespeare, 14–15, 84–85, 88, 98–100
    intaglio technique, 62, 64–65, *65*, 67
    printer identification projects (*see* computational bibliography)
    proofing, 37, 53
    relief technique, 39, 62–64, 67
    reprint continuities, 21–23, 26, 58, 74
    reprint departures, 29–31, 74–75
    of 1619 quartos, 14–15, 28, 38, 85–86, 100
    "states" *vs.* "editions," 68–69
    See also design; marketing strategies; rights-holders; typography
proofing process, 37, 53
provenance
    auctions and sales, 75, 97, 100, 101, 105, 115
    facsimile and composite copies, 111–14, *112*, *113*
    major collectors, 101–5
    and numbers of surviving copies, 98–100
    owner and reader inscriptions, 7–8, *8*, 46, *48*, *96*, 106–10, *107*, *109*
    private *vs.* institutional ownership, 100–101
    rebinding and trimming, 110–11
    slavery and colonialism legacies, 114–16
    value judgments and, 75, 104–5
    See also computational bibliography
Prynne, William, 35
    Histrio-mastix: The Players Scourge, 77, 79–80, 93–94
Puritan Widow, The (attributed to Shakespeare), 26–28, 88

quarto format, 15–16, 79, 81, 83–84

Rape of Lucrece, The (Shakespeare), 13–14
Rasmussen, Eric, 4, 139
Rawlins, William, 126
rebinding and trimming, 110–11
Reed, Isaac, 104
relief printing technique, 39, 62–64, 67
Richard III (Shakespeare), 14
rights-holders
    of First Folio, 16–17
    of Second Folio, 21
    of Third Folio, 23–26
    of Fourth Folio, 29
    title pages to recognize, 17, *17*, 21, *22*, 26
Roberts, James, 38
Roberts, Robert, 119, 126, 128–33
Rodd, Thomas, 112
Roman Actor, The (Massinger), 21
Romeo and Juliet (Shakespeare), 14, 17, 20, 98, 102
Rotton, Elisabeth, 108
Rowe, Nicholas, 105
Rowley, James, *The World Tost at Tennis* (with Middleton), *63*, 64

Saint-Omer library, 103
Saunders, Francis, 125, 131, 133, 138
Scornful Lady, The (Beaumont and Fletcher), 128, *129*
Scott-Warren, Jason, 106
Second Folio. *See* Folio, Second
Shadwell, Thomas, 28
Shakespeare, William
    friendships, 18
    making of, trope, 3–4
    See also entries at Folio; *specific works*
Shakespeare Census, 96–97
    See also provenance
Shakespeare Virtual Reality (VR) project, 5
Shepheardes Calendar, The (Spenser), 84
Sherman, William, 7
Shipp, Mary, 108
Sidney, Philip, 16, 80

Sir John Oldcastle (attributed to Shakespeare), 26, 28, 85, 88
1619 quartos, 14–15, 28, 38, 85–86, 100
skeleton formes, 53, 56
slavery and colonialism legacies, 114–16
Smethwick, John, 17, 20, 21, *22*, 23
Sonnets (Shakespeare), 102
speculative bibliography, 123
Spenser, Edmund, 16, 80
    Colin Clout, 84
    collected works (1611), 84
    collected works (1617), 84
    Faerie Queene, The, 84
    Shepheardes Calendar, The, 84
stab-stitching, 100
State Library of Hamburg, 102
State Library of Württemberg, 102
"states" *vs.* "editions," 68–69
Stationers' Company, 16, 21, 23–26, 142
Stationers' Register, 67, 68, 128
Steevens, George, 3
stop-press corrections, 53
Straet, Jan van der
    "Impressio librorum," *62*, 63
    "Sculptura in Aes," 64, *65*
Sutro, Alfred, 101

Taming of a Shrew, The (Shakespeare), 17
Taming of the Shrew, The (Shakespeare), 17, 108
Taylor, Jeremy, *Eniautos, A Course of Sermons*, 138
Tempest, The (Shakespeare), 2, 19, *129*
theater companies, 13, 14, 16
Third Folio. *See* Folio, Third
title pages
    intaglio prints for, 64–65, 71
    standard model of, 59–62, *60*, *61*
    type analysis of, 130–32, *131*, *132*, *133*, 138, *138*, *139*, *140*
    woodcut prints for, *63*, 63–64
title pages, Four Folios
    Droeshout portrait, four states of, 65, *66*, 69–70, *70*, 72
    in facsimile and composite copies, 111–13, *112*, *113*
    hybrid printing, 65–67
    imprints, 17, *17*, 21, *22*, 26, 74, 119, *131*, *132*, 138, *140*
    Jonson's poem facing, 42, *43*, 72–74
    textual and portrait layout, First and Second Folios, 42–44, *43*, 72–74, *73*
    textual and portrait layout, Third (1664 version) and Fourth Folios, 74, 74–75, *86*, *90*, 90–91
Titus Andronicus (Shakespeare), 14, 23, 38, 99
Tom Tyler and his Wife (attributed to Shakespeare), 28
Tragedy of Locrine, The (attributed to Shakespeare), 28, 88
Trettien, Whitney, 122
trimming and rebinding, 110–11
Trinity College, Cambridge, 108
Troilus and Cressida (Shakespeare), 82, 102
Two Gentlemen of Verona, The (Shakespeare), 23
type analysis, as concept, 120
    See also computational bibliography
typography
    damaged types, 56–58, 120–21
    English roman, 37, 125
    font size measurements, 37–38, 126–27
    italic type, 38, 51–52
    pica roman, 37–38, 82, 125
    pilcrows, 51
    textual errors, 7, 23, 26, 30, 53–55, *54*, 117, *118*
    typesetting process, 38–42, *40*, *41*, 53, 55, 56, *62*, 63
    type supply, 37–38, *39*, 55–58, *57*, 82, 120, 125
    typographic differentiation, 50–51
    See also design; computational bibliography

University and City Library of Cologne, 102
University of Glasgow, 110
University of Padua, 102–3
University of Pennsylvania, 107
University of Texas, 114
University of Wroclaw, 102

Valladolid seminary library, 103
Venus and Adonis (Shakespeare), 13–14, *99*, 99–100, 108

Wadham College, Oxford, 115
Walters, Henry, 101
Walters Art Museum, 101
Warner, Richard, 115
watermarks, 34, 36
Weiss, Adrian, 120, 121, 123, 130
Wellington, Richard, 139, 141–42
Wells, Stanley, 2
Werner, Sarah, 122
White, Edward, 14
Widener family, 101
William I, King of Prussia, 102

Wilson, John Dover, 20
Winter's Tale (Shakespeare), 102
Wise, Andrew, 17
Wise, Thomas James, 114
Wolfreston, Frances, 107–8, *109*
woodcut prints, 63–64
World Tost at Tennis, The (Middleton and Rowley), *63*, 64
Wotton, Matthew, 92

Wrenn, John, 114
Wycherley, William, 28

Yale University, 108, 115
Yorkshire Tragedy, A (attributed to Shakespeare), 28, 85, 88

Zurich Central Library, 102

THE PENN STATE SERIES IN THE HISTORY OF THE BOOK
James L. W. West III, *General Editor*

Editorial Board
Robert R. Edwards (Pennsylvania State University)
Paul Eggert (Loyola University Chicago)
Simon Eliot (University of London)
Beth Luey (Massachusetts Historical Society)
Willa Z. Silverman (Pennsylvania State University)

PREVIOUSLY PUBLISHED TITLES IN THE PENN STATE SERIES IN THE HISTORY OF THE BOOK

Peter Burke, *The Fortunes of the "Courtier": The European Reception of Castiglione's "Cortegiano"* (1996)

Roger Burlingame, *Of Making Many Books: A Hundred Years of Reading, Writing, and Publishing* (1996)

James M. Hutchisson, *The Rise of Sinclair Lewis, 1920–1930* (1996)

Julie Bates Dock, ed., *Charlotte Perkins Gilman's "The Yellow Wall-paper" and the History of Its Publication and Reception: A Critical Edition and Documentary Casebook* (1998)

John Williams, ed., *Imaging the Early Medieval Bible* (1998)

Ezra Greenspan, *George Palmer Putnam: Representative American Publisher* (2000)

James G. Nelson, *Publisher to the Decadents: Leonard Smithers in the Careers of Beardsley, Wilde, Dowson* (2000)

Pamela E. Selwyn, *Everyday Life in the German Book Trade: Friedrich Nicolai as Bookseller and Publisher in the Age of Enlightenment* (2000)

David R. Johnson, *Conrad Richter: A Writer's Life* (2001)

David Finkelstein, *The House of Blackwood: Author-Publisher Relations in the Victorian Era* (2002)

Rodger L. Tarr, ed., *As Ever Yours: The Letters of Max Perkins and Elizabeth Lemmon* (2003)

Randy Robertson, *Censorship and Conflict in Seventeenth-Century England: The Subtle Art of Division* (2009)

Catherine M. Parisian, ed., *The First White House Library: A History and Annotated Catalogue* (2010)

Jane McLeod, *Licensing Loyalty: Printers, Patrons, and the State in Early Modern France* (2011)

Charles Walton, ed., *Into Print: Limits and Legacies of the Enlightenment; Essays in Honor of Robert Darnton* (2011)

James L. W. West III, *Making the Archives Talk: New and Selected Essays in Bibliography, Editing, and Book History* (2012)

John Hruschka, *How Books Came to America: The Rise of the American Book Trade* (2012)

A. Franklin Parks, *William Parks: The Colonial Printer in the Transatlantic World of the Eighteenth Century* (2012)

Roger E. Stoddard, comp., and David R. Whitesell, ed., *A Bibliographical Description of Books and Pamphlets of American Verse Printed from 1610 Through 1820* (2012)

Nancy Cervetti, *S. Weir Mitchell: Philadelphia's Literary Physician* (2012)

Karen Nipps, *Lydia Bailey: A Checklist of Her Imprints* (2013)

Paul Eggert, *Biography of a Book: Henry Lawson's "While the Billy Boils"* (2013)

Allan Westphall, *Books and Religious Devotion: The Redemptive Reading of an Irishman in Nineteenth-Century New England* (2014)

Scott Donaldson, *The Impossible Craft: Literary Biography* (2015)

John Bidwell, *Graphic Passion: Matisse and the Book Arts* (2015)

Peter L. Shillingsburg, *Textuality and Knowledge: Essays* (2017)

Steven Carl Smith, *An Empire of Print: The New York Publishing Trade in the Early American Republic* (2017)

Colm Tóibín, Marc Simpson, and Declan Kiely, *Henry James and American Painting* (2017)

Filipe Carreira da Silva and Mónica Brito Vieira, *The Politics of the Book: A Study on the Materiality of Ideas* (2019)

Colm Tóibín, *One Hundred Years of James Joyce's "Ulysses"* (2022)

Melvyn New and Anthony W. Lee, eds., *Notes on Footnotes: Annotating Eighteenth-Century Literature* (2022)

Jeffrey M. Makala, *Publishing Plates: Stereotyping and Electrotyping in Nineteenth-Century US Print Culture* (2022)